Sin

Sinabada

woman among warriors

A Biography of the Rev. Sue Rankin

by

Laurel Gray

The Joint Board of Christian Education
Melbourne

Published by
THE JOINT BOARD OF CHRISTIAN EDUCATION
Second Floor, 10 Queen Street, Melbourne 3000, Australia

Scripture quotations in this publication are from the NEW ENGLISH
BIBLE, second edition © 1970 by permission of Oxford and Cambridge
University Presses.

National Library of Australia
Cataloguing-in-Publication entry.

Gray, Laurel, 1933–
Sinabada — woman among warriors.

ISBN 0 85819 736 7.

1. Rankin, Sue, 1897–   . 2. Women missionaries — Papua New
Guinea — Biography. 3. Women clergy — Biography. I. Joint
Board of Christian Education. II. Title.

266'.0092'4

First printed 1989

Acknowledgments: Permission for quotation from *We Lived with
Headhunters* by Ben Butcher (London, 1963) given by Hodder and
Stoughton Ltd, Kent, England; for quotations from *The Chronicle* (May
and June, 1964) given by the Council for World Mission, London.
The publisher acknowledges the assistance given by The Uniting
Church in Australia, World Mission, towards the publication of this
book.

Design: Jennifer Peta Richardson.
Typeset: Savage Type Pty Ltd
Printer: The Book Printer   JB/1655

Contents

There are many people who have helped me with this project by providing a place to work quietly and with their prayers and support. I would specially like to thank Herman and Linden Kalinin for introducing me to their word processor, Rosemary Gray for her typing help and Jean White and the Rev. Norman Cocks for their painstaking correction of the manuscript, and The Uniting Church in Australia, World Mission, for their generous assistance.

To
Sue Rankin
a mother in Christ to thousands

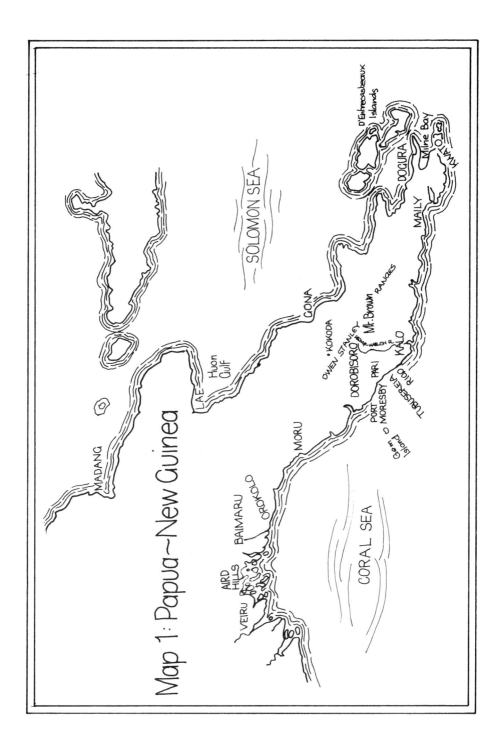

Map 1: Papua~New Guinea

Introduction

Sue Ellis Rankin is among the first ordained women, having been made a minister of the Independent Church of Wales in 1925. Tiny but indomitable, she pioneered women's ministry in the male-dominated society of Papua, where she worked as a missionary for fifty years. In a world where women did not own anything, not even their grass skirts, and where they were regularly beaten by their husbands, Sue became the highly-respected 'Sinabada' — 'big mother'. Under her loving and patient influence, Papuan women achieved a new status of respect and equality in their homes and their church.

As District Missionary, Sue preached to the Papuans and converted many. She brought them out of the darkness of their fear-ridden spirit-world into the Light of Jesus, the Great Spirit. She travelled many kilometres on long and often dangerous patrols, planting the Gospel — and the church — in new mission fields. Nothing, not even illness, increasing age or personal grief, daunted her when she saw a task she could undertake for her Lord. If one door closed to her, she looked for another to open . . .

A skilled linguist, she quickly mastered Papuan languages and then set about teaching the people to read and write in their own tongue. Never despising their culture, she strove to adapt all that

1

was good in it to the ways of the Christian Church. She brought great compassion and rare insight to bear in solving the most complex problems, including that of polygamy.

And the Papuans loved her. Not only had she brought them out of fear into the Light, she had taught them, healed them, consoled them, played endlessly with their children — her great passion — and sung with them in times of celebration. Even in old age, long after her official 'retirement', she continued to give herself to them unstintingly. When she left, well on in her seventies, she went loaded with honours. She was awarded an M.B.E. in 1972, the centenary of the arrival of the first London Missionary Society missionaries in Papua. A year later her alma mater, the University of Wales — where she was the first woman to gain a Bachelor of Divinity degree — awarded her an honorary M.A. degree in recognition of her linguistic and literacy work in Papua. Today, some twelve years after she left her beloved Papua, she is remembered with the deepest affection and respect across the length and breadth of the country where she worked.

She is remembered, too, in her native Llanfyllin in the hills of Wales, where she was born in 1897. When the people of Llanfyllin think of Sue Rankin (known to them as 'Suzie'), they link her with another distinguished daughter, recorded in their history. Two hundred years ago, Ann Griffiths was on her way to a social evening at Pengorphwysfa, the very farm where Sue was born, when her maid suggested that they go into the Pendref Chapel at Llanfyllin where a revival meeting was being held. Ann was converted, and became a gifted hymnwriter whose hymns are still sung in Wales. Sue was not spectacularly converted like Ann Griffiths, but she was nurtured in that same Pendref Chapel so that her faith grew till she knew without doubt that she was the Lord's child.

Sue tells of learning to walk with that steady, plodding pace used by the people of the hills of Wales, never hurrying, never slackening speed on the steep pinches. She was to climb the Owen Stanley Range with the same dogged determination. But long before she reached Papua, there were other mountains for her to climb. Could a Welsh farm girl, in the first decades of this century, gain the education she needed to become a missionary? She scaled that peak — graduating with a B.A. degree with honours in history and philosophy, and then a Bachelor of Divinity degree. And would the Papuan people accept an ordained woman as their minister? That turned out to be only a mountain of the mind. Sue attracted such respect that she experienced no constraints as a woman in Papua, and was readily accepted as both spiritual leader and 'mother'.

Sue's story is also the story of an exciting period of dynamic ministry by the Papua District Committee of the London Missionary

2

Society, and it is the story of her husband and missionary colleague, the Rev. Robert Rankin. But most of all it is the story of an exceptional woman — talented, sensitive, and full of fun — whose faithful and loving ministry changed the lives of many, many people.

Her story begins on that small farm in Wales before the turn of the century, in her own words.

Chapter 1

The little one

I was the fourth child of Frank and Jane Ellis. There were five more children after me, and when I was born my mother was grieving for five-year-old Gwen who had died following a fall. I was always called 'the little one'. My father said that, newborn, I could be put into a quart pot with room to spare. I was not expected to survive. The doctor was a frequent visitor.

There were seven of us at home during my childhood. My older sister, Margaret, lived in the town with our friend Mrs Bowen and attended the council school. My big brother Tom watched over me.

Our favourite occupation was comparing our heights. I was overtaken by each of my younger brothers and sisters till finally I refused to be measured, but stood on a chair to officiate with the ruler. We insisted that our parents also line up to be measured.

My earliest memory is of the doctor coming in at odd times, finding me indoors and shouting; 'Get that child out in the fresh air. She must not be kept indoors'. But I must have been lively enough; I played soccer with Tom and my younger brothers Enoch and Frank and the boys from the neighbouring farms. I became a tomboy. Although there was a birch rod up under the ceiling of the kitchen as a warning, it was never used on us. Mother gave us a tap with her hand if it was necessary.

Our small farm nestled into the hillside halfway up Alt y Gadair. The track from the town, Llanfyllin, to the hilltop passed just above our house.

The farm produced enough to feed the family but to earn money for shoes and clothes Father had to find other work. He became a plate-layer on the railway and a quiet leader among the railway workers. At harvest his workmates came to help on the farm. On the long summer evenings when it was light till eleven the hay-making or harvesting was quickly completed. During a break about eight o'clock, Mother served dinner to the workers.

On market days all settling up was done at the pub. Often quite a lot of money went in drinks. I was told that from the day I was born my father stopped drinking.

At harvest time he had been in the habit of providing a barrel of beer for the workers but as we children grew up it gave way to soft drinks. My father's friends respected his wishes because they knew of his decision at the time of my birth.

Christmas was a wonderful time. In our back kitchen was a fireplace big enough to burn logs, and a huge brick oven. On Christmas Eve the oven was lit and our neighbours brought their Christmas fare to be cooked; bread, cakes, mince pies, beef and sometimes poultry. The smell was marvellous. On Christmas morning we received an apple and an orange and a small bag of sweets each. Then the postman would pop in with our mail, share a snack with us and be given something to take home to his family.

After dinner on Christmas Day we children always climbed to the top of our mountain. Racing through the crisp winter air, we reached the seven small peaks at the summit which we named after the seven hills of Jerusalem.

A poignant memory of Christmas was the arrival of a poor tramp at our door one cold December afternoon. We took him into the warm back kitchen, sat him near the fire and fed him well. Mother said, 'No questions'. So we never learnt his name, just that he was not Welsh. Father fixed him a warm bed in our barn. Next morning we wished him a merry Christmas, gave him breakfast and off he went.

Our tramp turned up each Christmas for many years, getting a little older and thinner each year. He always went from us to the workhouse where the poor were given homes, and tramps could have a night's lodging and a feed in return for breaking a few stones for the roads.

One year when I had left High School we waited in vain. Our tramp did not arrive. Had he died? Did he have a friend to help him through his last days? Our grief for him cast a shadow over our Christmas fun.

I was very tiny till I was fourteen, when I started to grow. My brothers carried me to school every day till I was nine or ten. Down the hill we went from the farm and then up the slope to the county school. I insisted on walking past the county school. We often met the headmaster and said good morning. One morning he stopped me and said, 'When are you coming to my school?' I told him that I did not think my father would be able to afford the fees. However, I sat for a scholarship with the children from the surrounding villages and came second, so I was able to go to secondary school.

When we were small we bought sweets with our pocket money. As we grew older we saved up our pennies and often bought a Collins book for sixpence. Then we swapped books with our friends. There was a library at the school and a library at the chapel. We had plenty of English books to read but not many Welsh ones.

The boys knew that I loved to read. Out on the mountainside I had a special little tree. It was very leafy and when I was settled in its branches I was quite hidden. When I said; 'I don't feel like playing this afternoon,' my brothers left me alone engrossed in my book.

As soon as I arrived home from school on winter evenings I would curl up in a corner, shut my ears to the noise of the family around me, and read.

In the evenings Father allowed me to read while the rest of the family played games. When he had cleaned up after work and was sitting in his chair by the fire, we children would crowd around, two on his knees, one on each arm of the chair and the rest standing behind him. There were spills of twisted paper on the hearth used for lighting Father's pipe. As he told us a story or taught us a song he would bend over, take a spill, put it in the fire and light it. When he brought it up to light his pipe, that was our signal to blow. Out went the flame. We never tired of this game and Father rarely managed to light his pipe.

Sometimes Father would say to me, 'Tell us what you've been reading, little one'. I would sit on his knee and the others would sit around very quietly while I told them the story of The Basket of Flowers or The Lamplighter or Little Lord Fauntleroy. Next evening they would plead with me to continue the story. I became quite good at story-telling.

I often played at preaching. Staggering up the stairs with the big family Bible in my arms I would rest it on the curved rail of the first floor landing and preach to my imaginary congregation below. Many times the Bible fell over the rail while I was holding forth.

When did I get the idea of becoming a missionary? I can't recall a time when I did not dream of becoming a missionary. My friends took it for granted. Missionaries often told us their stories at chapel. Mrs Bowen's brother worked in India with the London Missionary Society. Each time he came home on furlough he visited us. We children were fascinated by his tales and the little carved monkey on a stick that he gave us. I had decided that God had called me to India.

Chapter 2

The chapel and the school

The Independent Chapel was the centre of the family's life and the Bible was the centre of the chapel. Education and recreation as well as worship revolved around the chapel. The children memorised many parts of the Bible in their Sunday schools, and at fellowship meeting after the evening service, each child would be asked to recite a verse of Scripture or a hymn.

The three succeeding ministers of the chapel during Sue's childhood gave her a great deal of encouragement. One elderly minister would pick Sue up and hold her high so that people could see her while she recited her verse.

Sue's first Sunday school teacher at Pendref Chapel was Tom Ellis, a carpenter. After the opening of Sunday school, the little children gathered round him to learn their Welsh letters. A sweet from his pocket covered with shreds of tobacco was the reward for learning the alphabet. Then the children proceeded to the next teacher who taught them syllables and short words.

As she sat in class on Sunday afternoons with the other girls, Sue's attention often wandered to the men's Bible study class in another corner of the Chapel. She longed to be able to study God's Word like that. She was intrigued by the method they were using called 'Higher Criticism'. At every opportunity she quietly listened to their discussion.

Later on Sue and her brothers and sisters started attending a second small Sunday school on Sunday mornings out in the country at a Chapel called Siloh. Sue loved telling Bible stories and often helped the teacher, Mr Davies, who had wanted to be a missionary. He encouraged Sue in her dream. One day he turned to her and said, 'If you're going to be a missionary you must start here at home. The Bible says, "Beginning at Jerusalem"; this is your Jerusalem'. This was a challenge to Sue who found it hard to talk to her family about her faith.

The young people were at the chapel every evening of the week except Thursday, which was market day. Wednesday was Band of Hope, where a young man from Liverpool taught them very thoroughly about the dangers of alcohol. Friday was the young people's meeting where they sang and recited and took part in games and quizzes. The young ones took part in concerts and eisteddfodau with their local choir, and played soccer, cricket, hockey, rounders, tennis, basket ball and rugby.

Mr Pentyrch Williams, the headmaster of the village school, had had a name for being very harsh in the early days before secondary schools when some of his pupils were boys eighteen years old. But Sue and her friends loved him for his gentleness. He was a deacon and local preacher at the chapel, who could keep the whole school enthralled with his Bible stories.

Sue was very proud of her Welsh heritage and loved the Welsh songs and history Mr Williams included in the curriculum. She regretted that English was the language of the school. Knowing Sue's feelings, when a famous Welsh scholar, Sir O. M. Edwards, visited the school the headmaster allowed Sue to have an interview with him. She found that he was campaigning for the inclusion of Welsh in the school syllabus. Her own experience of being taught in a language that was not her mother-tongue convinced Sue that if children became literate in their own language first they would find it much simpler to move to a second and even a third language. Sue has lived to see Welsh become the medium of instruction in many schools in Wales.

The time came for the tiny girl with the mop of auburn hair to start at the county school. She looked up at the honours board and said, 'My name is going to be on that board'. She was thirteen and there were forty pupils in the school. For the first time Sue made friends with girls and some of them are still her friends. Those children were all very aware of the sacrifices their parents had made so that they could be educated.

The people of Pendref Chapel supported the London Missionary Society. This mission was formed in 1795. The aim was to preach the Good News of Jesus Christ and allow the national people to develop their own type of church government. It was the first mission to work in China and Singapore and in most of the islands of the South Pacific, starting with Tahiti and Samoa, going to Fiji, Tonga, New Caledonia and later the Ellice group (now Tuvalu), and the Gilberts (now Kiribati).

The Rev. John Williams, an early pioneer to Tahiti, Samoa and the Cook Islands, was martyred in the New Hebrides. A line of ships named after him travelled the South Pacific carrying missionaries and supplies. They were called 'the children's ships' because the money to run each successive vessel in the line was raised by the children of Great Britain and other countries.

Each year Sue and her brothers and sisters took their cards from door to door in the village to collect from their neighbours for the *John Williams*. When the collection was complete Mrs Bowen would give the children a party as a 'thank-you' for their efforts. Sue received some beautiful book prizes for collecting. Her favourite was the Rev. Dauncey's book of Papuan pictures.

After matriculation Sue was employed by the Education Board on probation for one year and then accepted as an uncertificated teacher. She had a choice to make; whether to take teacher-training and teach for five years or to hold to her intention of going to university to train as a missionary. It seemed that Sue had no possibility of starting at university but she refused to commit herself to teacher-training. Having written to the London Missionary Society office in London she set the problem aside, leaving it to her Heavenly Father to solve.

Meanwhile the young Miss Ellis started work at the Anglican school in Llanfyllin. The traditional difference between church and chapel in the town was quite strong. 'Little Miss Independent' as the Rector called Sue, had difficulty understanding why the children had to learn the catechism and spend long periods kneeling up on hard wood benches to pray. Sue's pupils loved her Bible stories but the headmistress did not approve of her departing from those laid down in the syllabus.

At her next school, Clatter, in Montgomeryshire, Sue quickly gained the confidence of the older boys, refereeing their soccer games and skating on the pond with them in winter. She made two very close friends there, the one-armed station master whom she helped in his garden each Saturday, and the local carpenter who taught the young teacher some carpentry.

After six months Sue was suddenly transferred to Berriew. It was the middle of World War I. The headmaster was serving in France and his wife, also a teacher, was expecting a baby. Because of her ability to handle the big boys, Sue was placed in this school, near Washpool, which belonged to the local Education Authority. Again the rift between church and chapel came to the fore. Mrs Smith, the landlady, had two little sons who loved Sue. The older one trotted off to school with her each day. When the gentleman-owner discovered that Mrs Smith had a non-conformist boarder, she was evicted and moved to Liverpool where her husband was working in a munitions factory. Sue remained at Berriew till the Headmaster returned two years later.

While Sue was fully absorbed with her pupils a letter arrived from the L.M.S. Secretary for Wales, the Rev. Robert Griffiths, asking Sue to meet him at the station and travel a few stations on the train with him. He had exciting news for her. The London Missionary Society board members were considering her offer to serve as a missionary. When Sue gloomily said; 'I can't see any hope of saving my fees for university', Mr Griffiths encouraged her by saying, 'If God wants you as a missionary, the door will open. Just be ready'.

The door did open and things moved swiftly. A letter appeared in the Welsh Independent paper, asking whether theological colleges were open to women candidates. Encouraged by that, Sue's friend, Mr Davies, wrote to the principal of Bangor College, North Wales, asking for his ruling on the matter. The reply was; 'Yes, on the same conditions as men, that they have matriculated and passed a Scripture exam'.

Sue wrote to her minister at Pendref Chapel, the Rev. J. H. Richards, telling him that she wanted to enter college. She tells the rest of the story in her own words:

Mr Richards sent me to Bangor for an interview. I was excused the Scripture exam because I had been doing the Sunday school exams for some years. The next step was for me to preach at three different chapels. A report on each service was to be sent to the quarterly meetings of the chapels in the area.

My first service was at Pendref Chapel on 11 May 1919. Before the service my minister asked, 'Are you going to speak in Welsh or English?' I decided on Welsh because I knew if I started in English I would always preach in English. In the congregation that day were my brothers and many of the boys with whom I had grown up. I was nervous but people assured me that my old playmates were far more nervous than I! By 11 June I had preached at two more chapels and the quarterly meeting had sent my application to Bangor.

I was accepted, which meant that the Congregational Board would pay my fees, but I had to pay my own board. In September I left teaching and entered Bala-Bangor College of the University of Wales to commence an Arts course. Just before I ceased teaching, the teachers of the County had gone on strike for increased wages. I had never been paid more than fifteen shillings and sixpence a week. We were awarded an extra ten shillings a week and paid arrears. The Lord was already providing for me. My old headmaster often sent me a small

10

gift so that I could take my old school friends out to tea. We all boarded in the university hostel for three years.

For the six years of my course I earned my keep by preaching every Sunday. Some very generous churches in the slate quarrying area of Carnarvonshire paid three guineas for three services. That meant I had enough for my needs for the week and to buy a book as well. When once I preached at a place, I was always asked to come again. I guess it was the novelty of having a missionary girl to preach. My hostesses enjoyed over-feeding me. 'To keep me strong enough to go to the mission field', they said.

My principal became concerned about my working seven days a week, and gently suggested that I take a few Sundays off, although he acknowledged that he was guilty of disobeying that commandment, too.

I found the three years of the Arts Course easy and gained my degree with honours in history and philosophy. The time had come for me to enter Theological College. I was nervous. Would the men accept a woman student? At times I secretly hoped that I would be prevented from starting the course. The men students held a meeting in their common room and sent me a message of welcome, assuring me that they were happy to have me as a fellow student.

For a short while my entry to the course was in doubt. I found that I should have taken an introduction to Hebrew during my Arts course. Because of that omission I was not qualified to do the Hebrew text studies set. After a conference with the lecturers, it was decided that I should tackle the introduction and text concurrently. It was very hard work but I graduated, the first woman to win a Bachelor of Divinity degree from the University of Wales.

Because I was expecting to be sent to India I had long talks with some Indian students who were studying at the college and with an L.M.S. missionary from India who came to see them. But when the L.M.S. board accepted my application they appointed me to Papua. Perhaps the Lord knew that I was too hot a nationalist for India at that time! I knew very little of Papua except for the exciting stories of James Chalmers and my favourite Papuan Pictures Book written by the Rev. H. M. Dauncey. The L.M.S. sent me to Livingstone College in London to do a very short course in tropical medicine and a course in phonetics (linguistics).

Finally the day came when I was to be dedicated to the work. I felt that I should not be ordained before I went to Papua because the Papuan church might not be willing to accept a woman minister. The posters went out reading; 'Dedication Service'. I told the college staff and my minister that it was to be a dedication service, not an ordination. I thought I had convinced everyone.

The service was held in my own home chapel, Pendref, Llanfyllin, on 2 October 1925 during two days of missionary meetings. The Rev. Robert Griffiths spoke of his work in Madagascar and the Rev. Frank Lenwood, Foreign Secretary of the L.M.S., described his visit to Papua in 1916. On Friday afternoon the building was packed for my setting apart as a worker of the L.M.S.

My minister conducted the service and the charge was preached by my college principal. I was asked to tell how the Lord had prepared me and led me to offer for missionary service. The Rev. Ifor Huws brought greetings from my fellow students. I knelt and the ministers present prayed, dedicating me to the preaching of 'the glorious Gospel of the blessed God'. Mr Richards asked me to bring my ordination certificate to be signed. 'But I was not to be ordained,' I replied. 'Too late, it's done, my dear, we had all decided on it', he smiled. He produced a piece of paper which all the ministers signed, and later attached it to my ordination certificate.

It was very hard to keep on studying during my last year because my father became ill with cancer. He was eager for me to get my B.D. When I went home in June with my results he was very ill. There was a heat wave and the hay was ready to cut. Our friends rallied round to help get the hay in.

To the end my father was happy and loving and patient. Every evening our minister spent some time with him. On my father's last night Margaret and I sat with him while mother rested. Early in the morning he stirred. We asked if we should call Mother. 'No,' he said, 'she is tired, let her rest'. Suddenly his face lit up. 'What is it?' my sister asked, 'Can you hear the birds?' His face glowed with happiness. 'No, little ones, not birds'. His restful faith in those last hours comforted us all.

My brother Frank had emigrated to New Zealand with friends of ours. His wife and baby son were staying with us till he found a home for them. I was in Livingstone College in London in November when I was called home because my mother was ill. She had had several heart attacks, and died before I reached home.

People accused me of smiling at Mother's funeral. Yes, I did smile when her coffin was too long for Father's grave. My mind went back to our measuring. We children had been convinced that Mother was taller than Father but she must have kept her knees bent under her long skirts. I visualised my mother and father looking down at us, both so well and happy. My father slapped his knee and said, 'They found us out after all, Mama fach'. I thought, 'They have not lost their sense of humour'.

After my mother's funeral I found myself catapulted into a whirl of activity in preparation for my new life in Papua.

Chapter 3

To Papua

Sue was given a grant from the London Missionary Society to equip herself. Instructions came from Livingstone House (the mission office): 'Go to Vardons, the shipping agents, and order a year's supply of groceries'. A year's supply! Vardons provided her with a sample order which helped her to choose her provisions for the next year. They were packed and sent down to the docks ready to be loaded onto the *Cathay*, a P. and O. liner on which she was to sail to Sydney, Australia. Then followed a round of shopping for furniture, stationery, clothes, kitchenware.

It was very difficult for Sue to imagine the kind of clothes she would need in the tropics. There were certain rules, of course. Ladies must wear bloomers to the knee under their long skirts to protect their modesty when climbing into canoes and small boats. She needed hats, stockings, walking shoes, gloves for church and of course missionaries always dressed for dinner. The mother of one of Sue's former pupils who was a dressmaker sewed her several frocks. She continued to do this for Sue each time she went home on leave. God provided her needs through many people till she had the last book, piece of china, and saucepan packed and on board.

It was the maiden voyage of the *Cathay* and a very exciting experience for a young country girl from Wales. As they called at the various ports she saw for the first time people of lands and cultures very different from her own.

Her first impressions of Australia were the thrill of buying grapes for sixpence a pound in Perth, wonderful hospitality from people who supported the London Missionary Society in Fremantle, Adelaide and Melbourne, and the heat in Sydney. 'If the heat in Papua is like this, I won't be able to stand it', was her thought, but at sunset a southerly buster brought relief and a cool evening.

Sue was to travel to Papua on the *John Williams IV*, one of the line of ships for which she and her brothers and sisters had collected money in Wales. The *John Williams IV* was a sailing vessel with auxiliary engine that served Papua and the South Pacific islands.

While waiting for the *John Williams* to sail, Sue met Ethel Beckett who had also been appointed to serve in Papua with the London Missionary Society. Small and dark-haired with very fair skin, 'Becky' was a Sydney girl, a member of Woollahra Congregational Church who had trained as an infants teacher.

The *John Williams* was the lifeline of the mission. Captain Kettle and his crew made yearly visits to each mission station in Papua and the South Pacific with groceries and personal supplies for the missionaries and the various items of equipment needed for the mission work. They also carried South Sea missionaries and their families to and from Papua where they played a very important part in the work of establishing the church.

Some of the mission board members from Australia were travelling to Papua on this trip to attend the missionaries' annual committee meetings in Port Moresby (Papua District Committee or P.D.C.). Mr and Mrs Roberts, the Rev. G. J. and Mrs Williams, and Mr Gordon Searle (the treasurer or financial agent) and his wife were among the passengers.

They sailed on 22 February 1926. The voyage took eight days. It was a bit rough at times but when Sue found her sea-legs she began to enjoy all the new experiences.

One morning Sue was called on deck early. In the dawn light a long bank of cloud stretching along the horizon to the north hid her new home. As the *John Williams* ploughed on into the day the cloud dispersed to reveal a silhouette of ragged peaks and deep green coastline.

The passengers stood by the rail as the skipper brought his vessel through the reef and round the point into Port Moresby Harbour. They looked up at the town, a few weather-bleached timber buildings on the side of the hill above the wharf. The *John Williams* steamed further into the harbour and dropped anchor outside the marine village of Hanuabada. Hundreds of thatched houses stood with their feet in the waters of the harbour. Beyond them on a low hill, *Metoreia*, the large mission house built by Dr Lawes, and a cluster of other wooden buildings formed the mission station. Beyond, a steep range of grassy hills formed a backdrop to the tropical scene.

A launch nosed out from among the village houses and the new missionaries and visitors were welcomed by the Rev. J. B. and Mrs Clark. After unloading, the *John Williams* was to proceed west along the coast gathering up the missionaries for the P.D.C. meetings at *Metoreia*. Sue and Becky, keen to see more of their new home, after a day at *Metoreia*, re-embarked and sailed for Daru. First they called at Delena and Mr Dauncey joined them. Sue was delighted to get to know this gracious, gentle man who with his wife had worked at Delena since 1894.

The next port of call was Orokolo. As the party walked along the beach they met a family group of Papuans. Sue was very excited at her first meeting with Papuans but so frustrated at not being able to talk to them! Eventually one of the women gave her her baby to hold. The people were very amused as Sue cuddled and crooned over the little boy. As she patted him they gathered round and patted her. Suddenly she realised that the rest of her party had left her behind. Pointing along the beach she signalled that she should catch up with her friends. The Papuans took the baby and laughed at her antics as she ran off.

When they reached the island of Daru in the mouth of the Fly River the girls were introduced to the rich fruit of the mango. They were advised to eat it either in the bath or leaning over the veranda. Sue chose to eat hers lying on her tummy on the edge of the veranda, the luscious juice dripping through her fingers to the ground below.

During that trip Sue and Becky learned that Papuans did not regard people as adults till they married. An unmarried woman was a girl and an unmarried man was a boy. They also found that the L.M.S. worked mainly on the south coast of Papua. In 1890 Sir William McGregor, the Administrator of British New Guinea, had called a meeting of mission leaders in Port Moresby. He had suggested that different missions should agree to work in separate areas of the country. This was agreed to by W. G. Lawes for the L.M.S., George Brown for the Methodist Overseas Missions, and A. A. McLaren for the Anglican Mission. The Roman Catholic missions found themselves unable to join in this agreement, but apart from areas taken up by the Sacred Heart Mission the L.M.S. cared for the south coast of Papua. The comity agreement was very successful and enabled the three missions to work well together and use their resources wisely.

The *John Williams* returned to Port Moresby with her full complement of missionaries and Sue was initiated into her first Papua

District Committee. She found that her fellow missionaries were very much individuals, ranging from the gentle Mr Dauncey to some much more aggressive characters. The strong independence that enabled them to establish mission stations in isolated, inhospitable places and work out strategies for reaching new tribes sparked some very vigorous debates as the business of P.D.C. was dealt with.

One item on the agenda was the placing of new missionaries. Becky was appointed to Port Moresby as a teacher in the large school at Poreporena, part of the village of Hanuabada. There was some disagreement about where Sue should work. Some wanted to send her to Lawes' College at Fife Bay near the south-eastern tip of Papua to work with the student pastors. Others said that she would not be suitable for the college because she did not yet know Motu, the language of a large population round Port Moresby which had been adopted as the main language of the mission. They felt strongly that the students were not yet ready to have their lectures in English. The principal's wife had already summed Sue up as a Welsh nationalist who valued her native language and would be sensitive to the importance of the vernacular to the students. She carried the day and Sue was appointed to Fife Bay with instructions to spend as much time as possible in studying Motu. To become a full voting member of P.D.C., each new missionary was required to pass an exam in a Papuan language.

Dr Lawes had established a college for training Papuan teachers at Hanuabada in 1883. He often visited the marine village of Gabagaba and the Sinaugoro group of villages forty miles south-east of Port Moresby. In 1894 at Sir William McGregor's suggestion Lawes acquired land at Vatorata, three miles from Gabagaba. The college was moved, and the staff also cared for the Sinaugoro and Baravai villages which lay between the coast and the Kemp Welch River, forty miles inland. Some of these villages had become Christian and produced the first graduates of the college which became the centre of Christian growth in the area. Motu was the language used in the college and for preaching in the villages although it was not the local language, except in Gabagaba.

Every few years the area was drought stricken, causing much hardship and hunger among the villages. In 1924 the severe shortage of water caused Principal Turner to decide to move the college to Fife Bay. When Sue became familiar with the Sinaugoro area she always regretted that the college had not been moved inland to the banks of the Kemp Welch River, a beautiful site close to the foothills of the Owen Stanley Range.

All the buildings of the college at Vatorata including the memorial church were dismantled and moved to Fife Bay. A window in the church honours eighty-two South Sea island missionaries who died serving God in Papua between 1872 and 1900.

When Sue went to Fife Bay in 1926 the work of rebuilding the college was still going on. There were twenty married couples in residence at the college. The preparation of the women to be pastors' wives was considered as important as the men's theological training. They were taught to read and write Motu as well as simple hygiene, nutrition and housekeeping. For some Bible subjects they joined the men's classes. A primary school was conducted for the students' children.

Everything about Sue's life was new; the place, the people, the humid climate and the language. Fife Bay is one of many beautiful inlets on the south coast of the eastern tip of Papua. Fringed with rainforest and pushing back into the wooded hills, the land claimed from the jungle for the college campus and gardens was rich and productive.

Sue lived in the Turners' house at one end of the college while they were on leave. The Searles' house was at the opposite end. A Motuan student and his wife lived with Sue, and Mrs Turner had left four girls to board with her who could speak Motu well. Two of the girls were daughters of a pastor-cum-carpenter from Gabagaba who was helping to build the college. The other two also came from Gabagaba and had accompanied Mrs Turner when the college was moved. Every afternoon the girls took Sue for a walk and taught her the Motu words for her surroundings. It was a great game for the girls and a valuable lesson for Sue.

The new young missionary lectured in Bible subjects in English. Each evening she had a long session with two of the students preparing lecture notes in Motu. She had a copy of Dr Lawes' Motu Grammar but sometimes what the Grammar said and what her Motu helpers said was quite different. When Sue had a question she wrote to the Rev. J. B. Clark who, with Mr Turner, was revising the Motu Grammar. Mr Clark soon became aware that Sue was a very sensitive linguist. In June she went to Port Moresby for a short vacation armed with many more questions for him. He found that her thoroughness in tackling the understanding of Motu was bringing many details to light which would be very useful in his revision of the Grammar.

While in Port Moresby Percy Chatterton used Sue's gift for telling stories by asking her to tell fairy stories in English to the upper classes of Poreporena school. She was impressed with the children's understanding of English.

Teaching classes of students, their wives and their children, medical work, and language study filled Sue's very happy days. The students were encouraging her to start preaching in Motu but she did not feel quite ready. She felt much less self-conscious praying in Motu because then she could shut her eyes and not see people's faces!

After the college Christmas celebrations the missionaries left for Port Moresby for the annual Committee meetings. Sue expected to return to Lawes' College but instead was asked to relieve in Port Moresby for a year. Becky went to Fife Bay in her place.

A year in Port Moresby

Perched on a hillside above the Poreporena group of villages, the Port Moresby mission station was a noisy place. Every sound from the houses which stood in the shallows at the edge of the harbour drifted up the hill. Dogs barking, children playing, family arguments, reminded the missionaries that they were living among the people they had come to serve.

Each time a death occurred in the village the relatives wailed all night. Lying in bed unable to sleep, Sue could see in her mind's eye the unwashed, soot-streaked family sitting around the body, some rocking backwards and forwards and some cutting themselves with stones or knives till the blood ran to convince the spirits of their grief.

Sue was to act first as locum for Percy Chatterton the school master who was going on leave for six months and then for the Rev. J. B. and Mrs Clark, the district missionaries. Returning to Fife Bay she packed her belongings and reluctantly said goodbye. She then travelled to Port Moresby on the *John Williams* with the final year students who were to have a year of teacher training.

During the week-long trip the students confided in Sue. They were dissatisfied. They had gone to Fife Bay from Vatorata and had worked hard taking down buildings and relocating them. There had also been plenty of work to do making roads and landscaping the college. They felt that they had not had a full year's study. Knowing that the school week in Port Moresby was three days, Sue promised to give them some extra tuition during the year.

For the first six months she shared a house with Sister Gertrude Schinz. Two school boys who boarded on the mission station helped Sue in the house. Her work was to supervise the lower grades of the school of six hundred while Mr Clark worked with the upper grades. The hours were 7 a.m. to 9.30 a.m. and 2 p.m. to 3.30 p.m., the cooler parts of the day. Sue wrote the lessons up on the blackboard for each class and some senior pupils supervised the children's work. Pencils and notebooks and many other items were provided from the wonderful gift boxes sent by interested people in Australia.

Mr Clark had some untrained men to help him in the upper school. The Administration gave a small grant which enabled him to pay those helpers a little. The lower school was taught in Motu and learnt to read and write and do simple arithmetic. Although the children were supposed to start school when they were five or six most of them were nearer to ten. No records of children's birthdays or ages were kept by their parents. The children were happy and keen to learn and Sue had no discipline problems.

While she was working in Poreporena school Mr and Mrs Clark used the weekends and holidays to introduce Sue to the villages. She loved the trips on the launch *The Mauri*. At one village a man waded out to the boat to carry her ashore. He picked up the slight girl effortlessly. When it was time to return to the launch, he brought a companion to help him. 'Why two this afternoon?' asked Sue. The man replied, 'You were so heavy this morning you almost broke my back!'

During those long hours spent travelling on *The Mauri* the Clarks filled Sue's ears with stories of the Angas Inland Mission where they had worked before 1917. These tales made a strong impression on her.

When the Clarks went on leave Sue moved to the big mission house, *Metoreia*. There she looked after the school-girl boarders who came from distant villages. At that time H. M. Dauncey came in from Delena for medical attention. He stayed in the flat Sue had vacated so that Trudy Schinz could look after him.

Sue loved Mr Dauncey, who was about the age of her own father. 'He never looked down on people. He would ask me if there was anything I would like to get off my chest. "Come on, tell the old man," he would say. It was wonderful to have someone to talk to. I used to admire the way he addressed the Papuans as "natugu e" (my children). I thought it would be wonderful to talk to people like that if I lived long enough. Now I have lived long enough to say "my children and my grandchildren"!'

As well as visiting the villages of the district, Sue pastored the Poreporena Church which was on the head station near Hanuabada village and took the English services in Ela Church in the centre of Port Moresby. Ela was a small congregation. Although Sue preached at Ela in English she always wrote her sermon notes in Welsh.

The Poreporena deacons took a great interest in the new missionary and following their church services on Sunday afternoons would spend some time pointing out mistakes in her Motu and discussing how things should have been expressed. Sue did not feel very fluent in the language and was glad of the deacons' help.

Sunday afternoons were such a sleepy time for a church service that Sue changed the order and rather than having the Communion

19

at the beginning decided to have the sermon first when the people were wide awake.

When the Clarks returned from Australia on the *John Williams* at the end of the year a new recruit accompanied them. He was the Rev. Robert Rankin from Glasgow, appointed to Moru to replace the Rev. Pryce-Jones who had retired at the end of 1926.

Two or three days' journey from Port Moresby by boat, in the Gulf of Papua, Moru was a very lonely place. The house was in very poor condition, some of the posts eaten away so that part of the house had no means of support. There was no-one available to initiate Bob into the work. A few of the old men in the village befriended him but he found it very difficult to settle in to his new environment.

A letter to a member of the L.M.S. board in London dated 17 June 1929 reveals how lonely he was. 'May I suggest in passing one thing more . . . I understand there will be in the future some more men coming out. Should they enquire whether they ought to get married before coming out, please tell them *yes*. As a matter of fact all the recruits ought to be married. It is both for their own good and the good of the work as a whole'.

Meanwhile the Clarks' description of the Angas Inland Mission had caught Sue's imagination. This district east of Port Moresby stretched from the Kemp Welch River up into the Owen Stanley Range. There were many, many villages tucked away in those valleys and high on the mountainsides. The people were responsive, full of initiative, but also bound by fear and battling many diseases. A few of the people had become Christians before the Clarks left and they often wondered whether those young Christians had been able to stand against the pressures of their heathen communities.

Mr Angas of Angaston, South Australia, had given money for the establishment of inland work in Papua. All other L.M.S. stations were on the coast.

The Rev. Percy Schlencker and his wife were appointed to the Angas Inland Mission in 1901. They settled on a hill called Kalaigoro (Cockatoo Hill) near the Kemp Welch River. Pastors (then called teachers) from the Sinaugoro tribe who had trained at Vatorata assisted him. In 1911 Schlencker was transferred to Orokolo and the Clarks were sent to Kalaigoro. Mr Clark started pushing further inland and found many more villages a few days' walk up into the mountains. The Clarks moved their home from Kalaigoro to Boku, 1500 feet up in the Henty Range. From the clearing round the house the missionaries looked out over range after range of wooded mountains gradually rising to the jagged peaks of the Owen Stanleys. The people pointed out many villages perched precariously on the ridges of the range. The air was cool and refreshing and in the early mornings, mist filled the valleys.

The Clarks loved Boku and deeply regretted having to leave when, in 1917, they were put in charge of the very strategic Port Moresby district. There was no permanent missionary to take their place. In 1920 the Rev. Harold Short went to live at Boku. He was a very large Queenslander who had been a chaplain in the army in India. The people loved him but he found the walking in those mountains difficult. He spent some time relieving in Port Moresby and some at Daru and very little time at Boku. Hula, one hundred miles south-east of Port Moresby, was the Shorts' next posting and proved a very happy one for them.

When Lawes' College moved to Fife Bay at the end of 1924 the Sinaugoro people and the people of the Angas Inland Mission were left without a missionary. They felt very neglected.

As Sue listened to the Clarks she felt a real attraction to those inland people and their mountainous home. When moved to Port Moresby, Sue had expected to return to Fife Bay after one year but now she began telling people; 'I'm not going back to Fife Bay, I'm going to Boku'. At first her colleagues said, 'We can't send a single girl there'. But the seed had been sown and at the 1928 P.D.C., Sue was appointed to take charge of the Saroa and Boku districts. Miss Ethel Beckett was to work with her.

After the committee meetings Mr Short sent messengers to ask the Boku and Saroa teachers to come to Gabagaba as soon as possible to meet their new missionaries. He took Sue and Becky with him to Hula on the *John Williams*. He and Mrs Short prepared the two young women as well as they could for their new district. They talked about how to keep accounts, the payment of the teachers, preparing their kit for patrols and the desperate medical needs they would find.

Mr Short was anxious not to keep the teachers waiting for him at Gabagaba. He knew that they would have to carry all the food they needed for their trip to the coast. Just as he and Sue and Becky were ready to leave for Gabagaba on the Hula mission launch Becky became ill with malaria. Leaving her in Mrs Short's care, he and Sue made the three-hour trip back to Gabagaba.

They anchored within the shelter of the reef and Round Point. Sue could see the thatched houses of the marine village. One lone house had been built on the flat land beyond the beach. 'That is Nou Airi's house,' said Mr Short, 'He is a teacher and an outstanding leader among the Christians of the district. Here he comes now'. He pointed to a slight figure poling a canoe towards them. 'When you get to know him, ask how he became a Christian,' he suggested, 'It's a remarkable story'.

Sue saw a very, very thin man in a pink striped shirt with two

21

metres of purple cloth wound round his hips like a skirt and fastened with a belt. On his head was a floppy old khaki hat. Climbing on to the deck of the launch, Nou Airi took off his hat to greet Sue. He had only one eye. The young missionary found it very disconcerting to look at him. But she quickly forgot about Nou Airi's appearance. He was a very wise Christian and Sue came to depend on his advice in many matters.

They climbed down into the canoe and were taken ashore near the teacher's house.

Forty-four years earlier the Rev. W. Wyatt Gill, a missionary to Savage Island (Niue) had visited Papua to see how the South Sea teachers, many of whom he had trained, were doing the work of the Gospel and what progress had been made by the mission generally in the last ten years. He wrote:

We anchored at the village of Gabagaba . . . it has a population of 450. This is the third Swiss-lake-like village I have seen in New Guinea (a marine village). Ioane, a native of Savage Island, is their teacher. A fine plantation of yams, bananas, and sweet potatoes lies opposite to the village, the property of Ioane, who thus sets his flock a good example of industry.

Fowls and hogs are fed, and evidently thrive in these remarkable dwellings (over the water). This Papuan Venice consists of forty houses. Seven or eight miles inland, at the other side of the range, is Saroa, where a new station is to be started by our new Savage Island teachers.

Chapter 4

Her own district

Sue slid effortlessly into the life of the district. From the moment that she was lifted from the canoe by one of the men and set down on the dry grey sand of the beach, she was at home. As she walked up the beach to meet the line of teachers outside Nou Airi's house, Sue again wondered how the leaders of the church would accept a woman, or rather a girl, as their missionary. Her story is also the story of the pastors who matured under her leadership and encouragement: the men and women who followed God's call from the islands of the Pacific, at great sacrifice; the Papuan men whom she came to regard as fathers and brothers in the faith — Nou Airi, Timo, Humeu, Kiragi, Garikoto, Vanere Babona, Petero, Tom Nou, Mamata and John are a few of the great names.

Because the vowels of her native Welsh were similar to Motu, by this time Sue spoke Motu fluently. Having been taught by Gabagaba people she spoke with their turn of phrase. A young girl was standing curiously watching the new missionary. Sue asked her a question. The girl was so astounded that she did not answer but ran along the beach shouting 'She's a Motu girl, she's a Motu girl!'

Nine Papuan and two South Sea teachers were waiting to greet their missionary. It was clear they had no hesitation in receiving a girl as their leader. During the next twenty-eight years they respected her, but also cared for her like so many fathers. She was always carried from canoe to beach or river bank, never allowed to get her feet wet.

It was Easter-time, and Mr Short introduced Sue to the people of the village at a service on the beach. He also took her to the government station at Rigo and introduced her to Mr Vivian, the Government Officer in charge of the Rigo district. Sue told him that she expected her work to include being a missionary to the white people of the district as it had in Port Moresby.

Mr Short and Mr Vivian decided that the Anzac Day service would be a good time for Sue to meet some residents of the district. Among them were the Wyborns and their small daughter Nancy. Mr Wyborn worked for Mr English, a retired government officer who had opened a store near the Government station at Rigo.

Having noticed in Port Moresby that people often used their employment by the government as an excuse to have nothing to do with the mission, Sue stressed in her Anzac Day address that the King and his family always attended church and had family prayers and that Parliament in Great Britain always opened with prayer. She asked her audience to consider that the work of the missionaries and teachers, together with the work of the government, was for the well-being of the country.

Back at Gabagaba in her talks with the teachers Sue began to get a picture of the situation of the villages and the size of the area she was to care for. Ten kilometres inland from Gabagaba were the six Sinaugoro villages where the Gospel had first been preached about 1878. To the east towards Hula were the Baravai villages which had been looked after in recent times by Mr Short. Then there were those scores of villages stretching up into the ranges beyond the Kemp Welch River. Sue swiftly learned the names of the teachers and the villages where they worked.

Where were Sue and Becky to live? The missionaries and teachers considered the possibilities. The Gabagaba people thought they should live in their village, but there was no accommodation there except for the teacher's house and a small store, no church or school building. A small place up on Vatorata Hill, the old college site, about five kilometres from Gabagaba, was considered but Sue was still thinking of the inland people.

The teachers suggested that the new missionaries should make their home at Kalaigoro where Mr Schlencker had lived. It was near the Kemp Welch River on the side of a hill just above the village of Karekodobu. The teachers also made it clear that as soon as Sue and Becky knew the district well enough they should choose a place for the headstation that would serve the whole area. The Karekodobu people had been very disappointed when the Clarks moved the station to Boku. The church members all went back to heathenism.

After a few more days at Gabagaba helping Nou Airi give out the rations that were part of the teachers' salaries, and talking and praying with the teachers, Sue and Mr Short went back to Hula. Some of the teachers went to consult with the Karekodobu people about setting up the mission headstation at Kalaigoro. Repairs would have to be made to the old mission house and another house built for the two students and their families from Karekodobu, who had been preparing for college at Hula under Mr Short's instruction. They would now be Sue's responsibility.

On 1 May Becky had recovered sufficiently for the two girls to leave for Gabagaba. Nou Airi welcomed them and looked after them for a couple of days. Nou was a widower. In 1932 his son was one of the first group of Papuan men to be sent to Sydney for training as medical assistants. It was usual for widowers to stand down from the position of teacher till they found another wife but Nou Airi was so strong a Christian that he had been allowed to continue.

Leaving Gabagaba the two girls walked up the hilly, winding track through the bush to the grass-covered hills of the Sinaugoro area and the village of Saroa. A group of young men from Gabagaba carried their few goods. The people of the villages they passed through were quite indifferent to the two missionaries and their companions. At Saroa, Pastor Veniale and his wife Lesia of Tokelau Island welcomed them. They spent a few days in this village, which had been visited by Dr Lawes. The school was well run but there were few Christian people in the village. Sue was pleased to hear that Pastor Simona, also from Tokelau Island, would soon be returning from leave. He had already worked in the district for ten years.

It was a hot walk over the grass-covered hills from Saroa to Saroakei ('little Saroa') on the banks of the Kemp Welch River. By this time the party had grown to consist of the missionaries and their goods, the two student families and their belongings, and two little girls, Lucy and Kila. Their father was a teacher but their mother had died. Till he married again the teacher would return to his own village.

The group occupied a house at Saroakei for a few days because they had received a message that the house at Kalaigoro was not quite finished. The Saroakei house was new, having been built for a Samoan pastor who was subsequently sent home because he was too harsh in his treatment of the school children.

On Monday Mr Wyborn arrived in his truck, which was the first vehicle to be used in the district. He and his wife invited Sue and Becky to accompany them on a visit to the Watsons at Kokebagu plantation. As they drove along the river bank the girls could see row after row of attractive straight trees on the opposite bank, their trunks scarred with the 'v' shaped cuts of years of rubber tapping. After being poled across the river in a large canoe, their welcome by the Watsons was the beginning of a longstanding friendship. Many times Sue and Becky asked Mrs Watson, a trained nurse, for advice on the medical problems they encountered. If Mr Watson, who was an older man, thought his young wife was lonely, he would invite the two girls and Lucy and Kila to the plantation for a few days.

After that pleasant first visit to Kokebagu, a message arrived to say that the house at Kalaigoro was ready. The party gathered up their goods and walked the remaining fourteen kilometres to Karekodobu. The whole village turned out to welcome their new missionaries.

Sue and Becky were escorted up the hill to their new home and then a procession began, bringing gifts. There were all sorts of useful things; sweet potatoes and other vegetables, bananas, a chicken, coconuts and little brooms made from the coconut palm midribs.

Later Mr Wyborn brought the furniture and other heavy goods up the road to Saroakei, and the Karekodobu and Kware men man-handled them to Kalaigoro. The house was quite large with verandas on each side. The teachers had closed in the front veranda to form a large dining room and sitting room. Becky and Sue each had a bedroom at opposite ends of the house, the girls' room and bathroom were in between. They found that the repairing of the house had not really been completed and said that they were only alive to tell the tale because of their lack of weight and substance! The house had a beautiful view down the river.

The students' house was finished and then a house built for boy boarders. A small building for use as a church and schoolroom was put up right on the bend of the river.

Before their furniture arrived the teacher, who came from Boku, decided to go home for the weekend. Sue and Becky asked if they could accompany him. On that first trip up into the Henty Range they were not prepared for the sudden drop in temperature at sundown. They had taken only a light rug each and nearly died of cold during their first night.

When the village girls came to help unpack they asked Sue, 'Whose books are these? Your father's? Your brother's?' When Sue answered, 'No, they are mine,' they were amazed. One girl said, 'Oh, you are lucky'. Then pointing to her grass skirt, she said, 'You see this? It is not mine. Now it is my father's and when I marry it will be my husband's. All my life I won't have anything of my own'.

That changed with the coming of the Gospel. When the women saw that the men earned sticks of tobacco by carrying for the missionaries they asked if they could carry too and earn a New Testament or a hymn book. Sue kept an account book. When the

26

women had earned enough they were always very excited to receive their hymn book or New Testament.

A team

A routine of work began to develop at Kalaigoro. School classes were set up. The children found it difficult to concentrate on the three r's. One morning as Sue was teaching at one end of the room and Becky at the other, Sue turned from the blackboard to find the room deserted. A wallaby had hopped by and at once every child in the room was up chasing it. A few minutes later they came back from their fruitless hunt and work went on. Their teachers soon came to understand that catching a wallaby was much more urgent than school work!

Becky's main responsibilities were the school, store and book-keeping; Sue's the supervision of the teachers or pastors in the villages, and student-pastors and boarders on the station. Becky could sing well, a talent Sue did not have, but found Motu very difficult. One morning Sue found her puzzling over some Motu. The sentence meant: 'God is the One True God, isn't he?' The question tag, 'isn't he?' was translated 'ani?' In the dictionary one meaning given for 'ani' was a type of banana. Becky was concerned that the Papuans were saying that God was the One True Banana!

Many of the children were very sluggish mentally. In spite of a great variety of foods being grown, there were so many food taboos that the diet was probably inadequate. There were also people with elephantiasis, grotesque and shapeless swelling of the legs caused by the bite of a mosquito.

Treatment for malaria and tropical ulcers was given and generous doses of cod liver oil, a source of several vitamins, dispensed. Gradually a difference in the health of the people was noticed. But on one occasion the diagnosis proved wrong. Becky came running up the hill to tell Sue that a poor woman in the village was suffering from kidney trouble and was very swollen with fluid. Sue knew that if this were the case there was nothing she could do but decided to go down and see. She arrived at the house to find it packed with people awaiting the birth of a baby! Sue prayed with the woman and then signalled to Becky that they should leave. Halfway up the hill they both gave way to their embarrassed mirth.

Many of the people had swollen abdomens because they were infested with worms. A medical officer visited the village and asked the missionaries to treat all the adults and older children with a drug to wipe out the parasites. They followed instructions, administering the drug one evening. The following afternoon when the people returned from their gardens Sue and Becky went down to the village to see how their patients were. The people laughed ruefully. They said they had had a terrible doing from that medicine!

Once a quarter Sue walked down to Gabagaba to meet with the teachers. She held services and Bible studies, talked over problems with the teachers and gave out the quarter's supplies. Becky stayed back to run the school and do the daily work of the mission station. She had to hang on to her faith with both hands during those times when Sue was away. Because she did not understand the people or their language, Becky was often lonely and frightened.

Meanwhile Sue was learning a great deal about the thinking of the Papuans. On her walks to the coast she visited Kwalimurubu village, three kilometres from Saroa. There were about five Christian families in the village. The heathen chief always greeted her with great enthusiasm. On one occasion Deacon Guguna Kevau brought her the church roll book. She could see that many men had died over the years but there was no record of their widows' death or church membership. Sue asked what had become of them. The deacon replied that they had been suspended because they needed men to help them clear their gardens and repair their houses and there was only one way of paying for this help.

Said Sue, young and single; 'Why didn't you help them?' 'Don't you know what people would have said?' was the quick reply. 'Of course I do, but what does it matter what people say as long as it is not true? You had only to take your wife with you when you went to help'. That gave the church members food for thought. They began to look after the widows. That was how Sue became the champion of the widows.

On her way home from Gabagaba after one visit, Sue took a different route. From Saroa she went up across the hills. Not far from Karekodobu she came upon a small village on the banks of the Hunter River. A few years before it had been one of the largest villages in the district. When Sue arrived the teacher had just died and his widow and her sons were preparing to return to their home village of Saroa. Vaita, the second son, decided to go with Sue. He became her first schoolboy boarder.

Caught in a tropical downpour on one of her trips from Gabagaba, Sue had an experience which caused her to respect the Papuan people even more. Sue and the school children and ten men carrying supplies back to the mission station arrived at a heathen village on the banks of the Hunter just as the storm broke. The village appeared deserted. Everyone took shelter under a dilapidated house. The men made a fire and the group sat around and cooked bananas and rice and talked.

When the rain eased Sue and the children climbed the ladder into the house looking for a place to sleep. There was one large room with a plank bed towards one end. The boys put Sue's mat, blanket and pillow on the bed and rigged up her mosquito net. The girls were to sleep between her bed and the wall. The carriers said, 'Where can we sleep?' The area under the house was wet and muddy. Sue replied, 'Come up here, we'll manage to fit in'.

The whole party sat on the floor for prayers and a chat and then the men went down while the girls settled down to sleep. Then Sue called them to come up. The entire party slept in the house and when Sue woke at first light there was not a man or boy in the room.

The men from nearby villages were eager to help carry food supplies from the coast because they were paid, mainly with salt and tobacco but also with rice, cloth, knives and mirrors. Tobacco was about three cents a stick. The men were keen for a trade store to be opened but Sue and Becky knew that a venture like that would be very time-consuming. They decided to stock only enough goods to pay the carriers. Yams, sweet potatoes and bananas bought from the village augmented their own supplies of flour and rice.

Two young Australian patrol officers were very pleased to have young single girls settle in the district. They invited Sue and Becky to have a meal with them. It proved a disaster, the guests leaving precipitately when plied with liquor by their over-friendly hosts.

On the other hand, Tom Bowes, the manager of the government-owned rubber plantation, did not seem at all pleased to have two young female missionaries as close neighbours. The Watsons told Sue and Becky that he was in fact scared stiff. Sue pondered on ways of breaking the ice. Two small boys gave her the opening she needed. The ferryman took her across the river on his canoe and she walked up to the plantation. Bowes was supervising his labourers. His response to her greeting was: 'Good morning, do you want me for something?' Sue replied, 'Yes, I have a bone to pick with you'. 'What have I done wrong?' Bowes sounded quite upset. 'Two of my small boys were having a quarrel yesterday and I heard one say to the other: "No bloody fear!" ' stated Sue. 'Well, my friend and I don't use that sort of language so he must have learnt it from you!' He gave a half smile: 'Well, let's say you teach English and I teach profane?' 'Right', responded the young woman swiftly, 'but please go easy on the profane!' They both laughed and Bowes said: 'Will you come to the house and have a cup of tea?' 'I'd like that,' responded Sue. It was a beautiful big house. Tea was served from a beautiful little silver tea service which had belonged to her host's mother.

A friendship began. Each time Sue passed on her way to the coast she called to ask if there was anything she could bring Mr Bowes. Each time she was offered tea from the silver tea service. When the girls' house was in danger of collapsing they asked Bowes for help. He quickly arrived with some workmen and propped up the sagging structure.

Learning from the Papuans

'You are paying too much attention to the young ones and not enough to the older folks!' Mrs Vagi Dimoe had become a close friend of Sue and did not hesitate to give her advice. Sue explained that being young, it was easier for her to talk to the young ones. Vagi agreed but said, 'The message you are bringing us about Jesus Christ is just as important for the older people as the young ones, you know. We older ones need the church'.

She explained it like this: 'In the old days if young men went out alone to attack a village they would most probably turn and run when their enemies came out against them. It was always the rule that a few older men would go out with the young ones. Their experience would help the young ones to stand their ground and not to run away and so they would win. In the church, too,' she said, 'we need older people with a bit of experience to help the young'.

Vagi was from Gomore village near Gabagaba. One day she came to Sue; 'What can we do?' she pleaded, 'how can we make people realise that God wants action? They can all read and preach and pray in public but that's not enough. It's the living that counts. That's the only thing that will make outsiders believe'.

Sue went down to the coast a few days ahead of the teachers each quarter to help Nou Airi prepare for their coming. Account was kept of all goods the teachers had received during the quarter. Each teacher was allowed sixteen pounds a year plus one pound a quarter for each child. They were paid in goods. If the season had been good and there was plenty of garden food the teachers would have some money for clothes but if the season had been poor they took rice, flour, tinned meat and tinned fish. Because Nou Airi was a widower, he received three-quarters of the teacher's salary. Sue kept suggesting that Nou find another wife. One day someone whispered to Sue that Nou was interested in a widow at Saroa. Sue prompted him; 'I hear there is a very nice widow at Saroa'. The other teachers laughed and teased him. A week after Sue had returned to Kalaigoro, she heard that Nou had gone to Saroa and taken the widow Seketovo home with him. Sue was delighted at such an uncomplicated way of getting married.

When Sue had arrived in the district the teachers were in the habit of wearing black alpaca coats with their white ramis for preaching. She felt these were not suitable and far too hot for walking along the bush tracks. The stock in the store had run out and the teachers kept asking her to order more. Giving out the stores one day, Sue looked round for inspiration to distract them. She saw teacher Timoteo, a small man. His coat did not fit him at all. 'Timo,' she said, 'where are your hands?' Everyone looked. Timo's hands could not be seen under the long sleeves. The teachers all laughed and slapped him on the shoulder but they did not ask again for coats. A white shirt and black tie with their white ramis became the dress for preaching.

Nou Airi was a good teacher and having worked for some years as the pilot of the Governor's yacht, *Merrie England*, his spoken English was good. Sue admired his Motu and longed to be able to speak it as well. Each quarter Nou was waiting for her, armed with questions about his teaching. He wanted to know the meanings of words in the reading books, their pronunciation, how to teach a certain lesson. There were calculations he wasn't sure of but most of the questions were about the Bible. He and Sue spent hours going through God's Word together while she explained difficult passages.

After a week with the teachers, giving Bible studies and helping with school work, Sue sent the teachers back to their villages and then started off for Kalaigoro. As she walked along the tracks with her companions, she asked many questions. She thought about the villages of the Baravai tribe a little further south east, particularly Ginigolo and Gunugau, twin villages which were steeped in sorcery and fear. Old Pastor Solo who had cared for the handful of Christians there had had a very hard time. He had died and there was no-one to send in his place.

On her road were the Sinaugoro villages which had had pastors before the turn of the century. There were several men from Saroa, the main village of the group, who had trained as pastors at the college at Vatorata. The young missionary remembered the suggestion the teachers had made, that she choose a permanent site for a mission station when she knew the country better. Although the road to the river was very rough, there was one truck in the district. Perhaps later the L.M.S. would provide a vehicle for the missionaries. Sue was concerned at the heavy loads her friends from Karekodobu were carrying over thirty-two kilometres of hilly tracks.

If the station were situated at Saroa it would be on the road which ran from the coast, past the government station at Rigo five kilometres from Gabagaba, to the Kemp Welch River. When the road improved it would be easy to reach the river villages and start

31

from there on inland patrols. Sue filed these thoughts away and continued on to Kalaigoro visiting some of the Sinaugoro villages on the way.

The people of Gabagaba were the only true Motu speakers of the district. Many years before, some of the people of Tubusereia, between Gabagaba and Port Moresby, had become tired of the constant fighting with the nearby village of Pari. They had left and sailed east. They landed near Round Point and were met by people from Gomore who befriended them and hospitably offered them land near the sea. They accepted and formed Gabagaba village.

While Sue was at Kalaigoro, Gabagaba people often came to get timber to make canoes. The Karekodobu people allowed them to take timber, and gave them food while they were roughly shaping the logs for the trip down the river to the sea. In return the Gabagaba people promised to give them pigs and dogs when they came to the coast. But when the river people arrived at Gabagaba the people would ignore them till at last they were compelled to go home without their payment. Sue was annoyed to see this happening. She spoke to Nou Airi, asking if he could do something. 'I'll find out who the people are,' he promised. He was able to solve the problem.

On one occasion when some Gabagaba people were working on the river bank at Kalaigoro preparing canoe logs to float down the river, they asked permission to sleep at the mission station. There was an old store opposite the missionaries' house which Sue and Becky allowed them to use. Each evening just before sunset they arrived to cook and sleep. One evening as soon as they arrived someone began to scream. Sue went across to investigate and found a young woman tossing and screaming on her mat. Thinking of sunstroke, Sue asked the people what was wrong. 'When we were passing through the village a spirit grabbed her,' they explained. 'Oh, no,' said Sue, 'There are no spirits, I'm sure it must be sunstroke, I'll give her some medicine to help her sleep'. The people protested that a spirit was causing the trouble. Sue would not listen. The people's faces changed. It was as if a door had slammed in her face. Sue was outside and they could no longer communicate.

She went to her house feeling very confused. Were there really evil spirits? She got out her Bible and read all the stories where the Lord cast out evil spirits. Did Jesus believe in them? Sue did not know, but she saw that he talked to the people in ways they could understand. In trepidation she went back to that house and said to the folks, 'I'm sorry, I did not understand. Will you tell me again?' They explained again how, as they were leaving the village, a spirit grabbed the lass and she began to scream. They sat and talked about evil spirits and the sort of things they did. The girl was still very hot and restless and screaming off and on. Eventually they allowed Sue to pray for her and then give her a sedative. After a while she slept. The next day her mother watched over her while she rested and Sue took them some food and the following day she was well enough to walk back to the coast. Sue had learned a lesson: never argue about the people's beliefs or deny them offhand, but meet the people on the grounds of their beliefs as Jesus did.

The village people said that Gogina, a village youth, was possessed by an evil spirit. He roamed around in the bush and hills, not eating or sleeping at home. He came to Sue and said, 'The spirit said if I came to you I could sleep'. She took Gogina to her bedroom and settled him on a mat with a blanket and pillow. He slept for some hours and then walked off. He often came to the mission station after that. The school boys were a bit afraid of him. Once or twice Sue tried to give him food but he would not wait, just pulled green bananas off a bunch. The school children were horrified that he ate them skin and all.

One day the students and boys were repairing the walls of a house. They had taken off the old thatch and were tying midribs of sago fronds together with cane to make the new wall. As they worked they laughed and talked. Sue, who was working in her room, suddenly noticed that the chatter had stopped. She went out to find the students and boys all working frantically and Gogina standing over them with a poised spear. Going over to him she said, 'You won't hurt my boys, will you?' He kept his eyes on them and whispered to her, 'I'm only making sure they work'. Sue stayed to watch. The wall was finished in a very short time and then Gogina wandered off.

The young man continued to visit the mission station and often had a rest in Sue's room. One day someone in the village sent word to say that the spirit had left Gogina and he felt sick. Sue went down with food and medicine for him and found him very weak. Over a few months he gradually regained his strength.

At the end of 1928, Sue and Becky arranged a Christmas gathering at Kalaigoro. Coastal people and inlanders came. There were feasts, games, races, singsongs and church services. As long as the men were divided into village groups all went well but then they wanted a coast versus inland tug o' war. The coast men won. They made too much of their victory and the inland men picked up their spears. As one of the Karekodobu men rushed forward with his spear raised, Sue grabbed his arm to hold him back. After the fracas, Sue spoke to the teachers. 'This friction between coastal and inland people is not good. We want to teach the heathen people that Jesus came to bring peace'. One of the teachers assured Sue that there was nothing to worry about. 'Every Christmas we have

33

a fight,' he said, 'but this year there was no blood, so it was all right'.

When Pastor Simona returned from leave he and his wife went to live at Karekodobu. When he took up the duties of preaching and school classes at the mission station, Sue and Becky were at last free to visit the inland villages. They sent runners ahead to tell the people they were coming, packed their food, cooking utensils, medicines and tobacco to pay the carriers and called for carriers from the village to accompany them.

It was more than ten years since the inland Christians had had any pastoral care and the girls wondered what they would find. First they entered the territory of the Kware people who until recently had been the enemies of the Karekodobu tribe. Not far along the track their guides stopped at an intersection. They said that the name of the place was Deba Rore which meant a row of heads. One man explained that it was the site of the last big fight between the Karekodobu and Kware people. He told how they had cut off the heads and set them up in a row. The skulls were still scattered in the bush near the track. It was the faithful work of the Schlenckers and the Clarks that had brought the peace of Jesus Christ to those people.

From Deba Rore the track began to climb. To reach Gevera Goro the party ascended a very steep hill called Gode Sese. They went up a short distance and had to prop themselves against a tree to get their breath, then on again and rest again. It seemed never-ending. At the top Becky said, 'A far better punishment than hell-fire would be to have to climb a hill like this for ever and ever!' The girls nick-named Gode Sese, 'Hades Hill'.

Vaita had appointed himself as cook to the party. As soon as they arrived at Gevera village he lit a fire and heated water so that they could have a wash. He then proceeded to cook their meal. The girls were camping in the pastor's house which was unoccupied. Feeling refreshed, Sue went down to talk to the village people who were sitting round watching the party set up camp. She found that the men spoke Motu but she could not communicate with the women at all. They looked so stolid and unresponsive. An old gramophone was among the things Sue had brought with her. She put on the record of Harry Lauder's *Laughing Song*. Harry Lauder laughed, Sue and Becky laughed, and then the people joined in and everyone laughed and laughed. At last they were thawing out.

Becky gathered the children together and taught them some games; skip tag, in and out the windows, cat and the mouse. Gradually some of the men joined in and at last everyone was trying. They could not skip but would try and then roll over on the ground laughing. They quickly lost their fear of the white women.

34

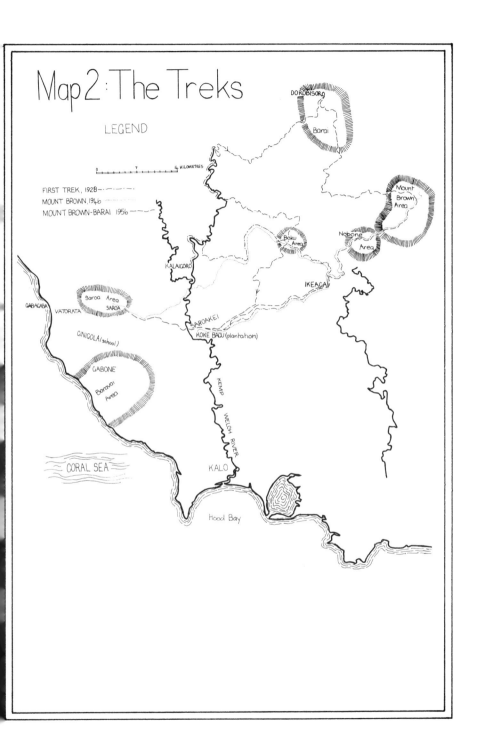

On that first visit the people appeared to have forgotten the Motu and Sinaugoro hymns taught them by the Schlenckers and the Clarks, and the prophet songs or perovetas which the South Sea pastors had brought with them. Late in the afternoon the women and children went home to prepare their evening meal. In the evening Sue told the men who were still sitting round, a Bible story, said a prayer, and then the whole party settled down gratefully for the night. Kone Binani, one of the pastors, continued with Sue and Becky on their patrol. He was a man of great influence, a born leader. Although he had very little education, Kone had worked hard in many of the inland villages.

At first the carriers expected to carry Sue and Becky. Evidently they had carried Mrs Clark. They warned Sue that in some of the steep places she would need help. She said, 'Well, you can push me, I don't want to be carried'. Sue wore heavy walking shoes with studs in the soles which gave her confidence on the steep muddy tracks, but Becky chose to wear sandshoes which were often very slippery. Coming down the steep pinches, a man would hold Sue by each arm. Becky did not like being held like this and often Sue had to help Becky while a Papuan man held on to Sue!

The next stop was lovely Boku, the centre of ten villages. There was a large house built by Mr Clark. From the veranda Humeu, the teacher, pointed out the Spirit Mountain called Durigoro or Mount Barron. Conical, the extinct volcano was a 3,000-metre peak feared by the people as the abode of the spirits of the dead.

Humeu was faithfully teaching the children in school each day and a few people turned up for Sunday service but they shamefacedly told Sue that every church member except one woman had gone back to their old heathen customs of dancing and feasting. Sue asked the woman to persuade the people to come and talk to her. They came and she gently told them that it was not too late for them to come back to Jesus, God would forgive them and receive them again as his children if they would come back to him. She told them that on her next visit she would see how many were ready to become part of the church fellowship again.

Becky and Sue spent several days at Boku encouraging Humeu, talking to the people, treating sores and malaria, and visiting some of the nearby villages.

One Saturday afternoon they were standing on the veranda enjoying the majestic scenery of mountains, ridges and deep valleys, when they caught sight of men stealing towards them through the tall grass. They were dressed in all their finery of warpaint and head-dresses and shells and with great spears in their hands. Becky said, 'What will we do?' Sue, terrified, replied, 'We can't do anything, we'll just have to stay put'. The warriors came shouting out of the grass and hurled their spears into the ground in front of the two girls. Then they straightened up and laughed. 'That's what we would have done long ago, but we don't do it today'. Sue and Becky took a long breath of relief and, picking up some tobacco for the men, went down onto the grass and sat down to talk to them. They learned a great deal by chatting to the people in a leisurely fashion, often through an interpreter who had learned Motu while working on one of the plantations.

The missionaries continued on their way to the Wiga group of six villages. The teacher had been moved to another village and only one man, the village policeman, was still faithful to Jesus Christ.

The next community was the Ikeaga tribe. Here Sue found things much more encouraging. The people happily joined in the games and prayer times. The chief and his wife gave the missionaries a great welcome and accompanied them from village to village with a great crowd of their people. A group of young men who had just returned from a plantation attached themselves to the party and became carriers for the remainder of the patrol. They spoke Motu and acted as interpreters. Their leaders were named Johnny and Jimmy.

The main village for the Ikeaga tribe was Dakeva Komana. There had been no pastor there for some time but two of the young couples from the village were studying at Lawes' College. Sue and Becky camped in the empty teacher's house. They followed the same pattern in getting to know the people and, after the evening meal and prayers when the women and children had gone off to bed, sat and talked to the men. They talked about the church, why the missionaries had bothered to come, the ways of white people.

During that first visit to Ikeaga, Sue met Wala Duma. He was a noted person in the village who had been one of the first to become a church member, though he had four wives. The missionary did not tell him to get rid of his wives, but made him a deacon. Wala had been well-known because when he first became a Christian he was brave enough to go into the enemy villages with no spear or club in his hand to tell the Good News. Most of the villages were built on ridges or hillsides with high timber stockades round them because they were all enemies and needed to defend themselves.

But when Sue arrived, Wala Duma too had gone back to the heathen ways. One day he and Sue went for a walk. They came to a tumble-down house, sat on the steps and he told this story (Papuans often explain things through stories):

In one village there was a pig. This pig had a master. The master was very fond of the pig and the pig was very fond of his master. The master talked to him, looked after him, went

37

for walks with him, and they were very happy together. Then one day the master went away and the pig was very lonely because he had kept very close to his master and hadn't made friends with the other pigs. But the pig cheered himself up by saying, 'Never mind, my master will come back soon and then I'll be happy again'.

But one day went by, and another day, then one week, and another week, and still the master didn't return. By this time the pig was really lonely and hungry, too, with no-one to think about him. One day, out in the bush where he was looking for food, he met a bush pig. 'Why are you looking so sad?' asked the bush pig. 'My master has gone away and I am very lonely', replied the pig. 'Come into the bush with me', said the bush pig, 'It's lovely here in the bush, there is plenty of food and there are good places to sleep'. 'Oh, I couldn't do that', said the pig, 'if my master came back and couldn't find me he'd be so sad'. But his master didn't come back and one week after another went by and then one day when he was feeling very sad and lonely, he listened to the bush pig and went off with it into the bush.

'That is my story', said Wala Duma, 'I was just lonely'.

Wala Duma came back and others with him and soon a little fellowship came into being. They had not heard enough of the Gospel. They had not understood that the full story of the Gospel was that they were never really alone, that Christ was with them everywhere. The lamp of the Gospel had been lit but had not been kept burning. One by one the Christians had gone back to their old ways.

As the young men from Ikeaga went from village to village with the missionaries they heard Sue telling the people about Jesus Christ, how he had died and risen again to set them free from fear of spirits and death and sorcery. Kone Binani had been their teacher and had taught them to read Motu. One day they said to Sue, 'We would like to become Christians but we don't want to cut our hair'. They had beautiful big bushes of hair of which they were very proud. 'Who said you had to cut your hair?' Sue asked. 'That is the sign of a Christian,' they replied. Sue explained that being a Christian had nothing to do with their hair and told them the story of Samuel looking for a king among Jesse's sons, how Samuel turned down one after the other of those handsome young men and then chose the youngest, a scruffy lad come straight from looking after the sheep. 'You see,' she explained, 'it wasn't their appearance God was looking at but here (pointing to her chest), to see whether they would listen to God's Word and obey him'. After that, as they went from village to village Sue and Becky heard the youths telling the people, 'She says it is not our hair God looks at, but our minds'.

Ikeaga was the last of the inland tribes which had been opened to the Gospel, so Sue and Becky returned to Kokebagu plantation. The Watsons welcomed them, and they luxuriated in a hot shower, a delicious meal and a comfortable bed before they made their way back to Kalaigoro.

Becky had found on that trip that she disliked patrolling whereas Sue revelled in the contacts with the people and even the discomforts. She and Sue were not to remain colleagues much longer. Temperamentally they were opposites; Sue gregarious, Becky prone to go for days just 'not talking'. Their views of Papua and the Papuans and the work they had been appointed to do were quite different. Becky decided that after her leave she did not wish to return to Kalaigoro. She asked to be transferred to Fife Bay.

Chapter 5

Rebuilding the inland church

Sue returned from that patrol, her heart torn for the pastors and Christians who had remained so faithful and for the many who had fallen away. There were four centres with teachers: Kalaigoro, Roroganomu in the Kware tribe, where Kone Binani was working, Boku with Humeu, and Saroakei near Kokebagu on the Kemp Welch River. In the coastal section men were working in six villages and two couples from Karekodobu and two from Ikeaga were training.

Each quarter Sue visited those inland villages. It took about three weeks, staying a day or two in each village. Her visits were looked forward to and when she arrived the people would be in a holiday mood, the village street decorated with palm leaves and hibiscus. They would be eager to play the games she had taught them and to sing songs and hear the Bible stories. They were learning that the Christian way was a way of fun and laughter and joy.

Sue had met the two students from Ikeaga, Mamata and Nanuna, at Lawes' College, Fife Bay. Mamata had told Sue that when he was a lad his father woke him one evening and said: 'Come and hear your grandfather preaching'. The people of the village had gathered together to hear the chief, Bagu Verave, speak to them. He said, 'I have heard that down in Saroa they are no longer fighting. Would you like to live like that, with no fighting?' The people shouted; 'Yes, we would.' The chief spoke again. 'I have heard that at Saroa they are not so afraid. They don't have their spears and clubs beside them when they sleep. Would you like to be able to sleep like that?' Again the people shouted; 'Yes, we would'. The chief then said: 'I'm told that they live like that at Saroa because they are learning a good story. Would you like to learn that story?' Again the reply was; 'Yes, we would'. Then the chief said, 'Very well then, bring your gifts tomorrow and we'll send word to Maino Kiragi (a pastor from Saroa working in one of the Kalaigoro villages). We will ask him to see the missionary and ask for someone to come here and teach us. But,' said the chief, 'you must always remember that this teacher will come, not because he wants to come, but because you want him. So you must promise me now that when he comes you will listen to him, respect him, obey him and supply his needs. Will you?' The people shouted; 'Yes, we will!'

They sent men to see Maino Kiragi and Mr Schlencker at Kalaigoro and then went to Vatorata to see Dr Lawes at the college and ask for a pastor for the Ikeaga tribe. Dr Lawes promised them that when the *John Williams* arrived with teachers from the South Sea Islands, one would be sent to Ikeaga. A Niuean man and his wife went to Ikeaga, which is why the people knew some Niuean prophet songs, but they did not stay. They found the mountain walking difficult and could not get used to the mountain people's methods of baking vegetables in the ashes, no coconuts and lack of fish.

Remembering Mamata's story, Sue realised that the Ikeaga people had been hungry for the Gospel for a long time.

At the end of that year there were quite a few little groups of Christians meeting to worship God in the inland villages, but mostly without anyone to lead them. Then Nanuna was sent home from college having failed in his exams. He was sent to work with the Wiga tribe. Sue did not find him a 'drop-out' but a very dedicated pastor. The people told her that he went and worked with them in their gardens and as he worked explained some part of the Gospel story to them. Very soon there were many people from the Wiga villages asking to be baptised.

Meanwhile, that same group of youths from Ikeaga still accompanied Sue on her patrols to the coast and inland. Then they said, 'We would like to become church members, but we don't want to give up dancing. Life would be very dull without dancing'. Sue decided to call a meeting of pastors, church members and any interested in becoming Christians. She sent word to the coastal and inland villages and asked the people to come to Kalaigoro.

They came in far greater numbers than Sue had expected. When she saw them all she was quite afraid. There was such a crowd of young men with long hair. How could she ever control such a

41

crowd if things went wrong? They started the meeting with prayer and then Sue asked the young men to start the discussion. One spoke and a pastor replied. Another young man spoke and a pastor replied. So it went on. This was what they call the 'Melanesian Way'. There was no disorder, no hot temper, just quiet, reasoned talk. After a couple of hours of discussion Nou Airi, the senior pastor, rose to his feet.

He pointed out that the dancing and feasting were closely connected with the worship of ancestral spirits and that if they chose to follow the Great and Holy Spirit, God, they could not go on worshipping the ancestral spirits. He reminded them how often there was trouble in a village after a dance. He concluded; 'Dancing is a part of spirit worship and has much immorality connected with it. Let us give it up now and one day when all its old connections are forgotten we can revive the dancing as something we can all enjoy'.

The young men accepted that and within a few months asked to be baptised into the church. They were all very enthusiastic about sharing their faith in Jesus. John trained as a pastor, one boy became a lay pastor and some became deacons in the church. John was not a scholar or a fluent preacher. His text was always 'Let your light so shine . . .', but he was one of the most respected and loved of the pastors in the district till he died in 1979.

One morning after a meeting on the veranda of the teacher's house at Saroakei, Sue picked up an unsmoked cigarette from the floor. It was rolled from newspaper and trade tobacco. 'Look Babona,' she said to the teacher, 'somebody has left a cigarette'. Babona replied, 'This is a dangerous one, Sinabada. I am sure it is poisoned. No-one smoked it. Somebody wanted me or someone at this meeting to smoke and die. Look, I'll show you'. He opened up the cigarette. Sue saw that the trade tobacco was there in short fibres but in between were little flakes of bark. He said, 'See, that is a certain tree. Whoever smoked that cigarette would die. You have heard rumours of people being poisoned. That's one way of doing it. They vomit and have diarrhoea but you can't prove anything'.

Sue had heard many stories of unexplained deaths. A young man who came back to the village with plenty of money after working on a plantation would commit adultery with one of the married women. In a short time he would be dead. Occasionally a man would be coming down to the government station to report a misdemeanour, and would die on the way. If the people did not think that a person had received the sentence he deserved in a court case, he would mysteriously die a short time later of 'pneumonia'.

On returning to Kalaigoro after one of her inland patrols Sue found a letter from Bob Rankin waiting for her.

The young Scot from Glasgow who had arrived with the Clarks when they returned from leave in 1928 suggested in his dry, restrained way that he and Sue should 'join forces'. His letter explained that as a single man he was very limited in the mission work he could do. Single men were regarded as boys in Papua, not as adults.

Bob's proposal took Sue by surprise. She had no thought of getting married. Having grown up with brothers and gone to a college where she was the only woman she was quite at ease working with men. She was very settled in the Boku-Saroa district and had been accepted by the people. Sue looked at the young Ikeaga men who had again accompanied her on patrol. They were growing in their faith in Christ. 'No,' she thought, 'I can't leave them'. Her reply to Bob was; 'No, thank you, I'm not interested'.

He never admitted to receiving that letter but continued writing to Sue and, when they met at P.D.C., filled her ears with the desperate needs of the Moru people.

Sue and Becky had almost completed their first term of four years as missionaries. They were due for six months' leave. Sue and the pastors had made the decision that when she returned from leave, the headstation would be moved to Saroa. Although the boarders loved the fishing and swimming at Kalaigoro, most of the boys were from the Sinaugoro villages and would be able to live at home and walk to school each day.

Towards the end of that year Sue travelled down the Kemp Welch River by canoe to Kalo and walked across Hood Point to Hula. There she met a new missionary who had just arrived on the *John Williams*. Sue and Gwen Milne became very close friends at once. On arriving in Port Moresby Gwen became ill with diphtheria and was sent home to Tasmania to recover.

Sue had not had much time to visit the Baravai tribe except for Ginigolo and Gunugau, so before she went on leave the young men from Ikeaga accompanied her on a walk from Saroakei to the Baravai villages. It was a hot, dry walk through the tall Kunai grass on the hills near the river. When they arrived at Gamoga the people were all busy thatching. The chief was in mourning because his wife had died, and was therefore covered with soot. The people all came down from the roof to welcome Sue and took her into the chief's house and gave her a box to sit on. They cooked food for the carriers and gave Sue a few bananas, not being sure what this white girl ate. While she was eating they sat around and talked, particularly discussing her clothing. They named the various garments; stockings, shoes, singlet, dress, and then one of the men said she would be wearing 'piribou', a word used right through the South Seas for pants of any kind. The women looked utterly disgusted and shook their heads. The man said, 'I know'. The woman next to Sue very gently lifted up her skirt and sure enough, there they were! Not a word was said, the man gave a snort and stuck out his tongue. Sue stifled her laughter and pretended that she had not understood what was said.

Leaving Gamoga the party went on to Tauruba, the largest village of the group. Sue had been warned by Mr Turner that the people of Tauruba were very reactionary and soon drew anyone who became a Christian back into the old ways. He said that any pastor appointed there would have a difficult time. Pastor Fatuatau, a Niuean, was a very gentle man and when Sue arrived she found that his wife had a great cut on top of her head. As Sue cut away the hair round the wound and stopped the bleeding, she heard the story.

The pastor's house was situated just below the road which led from the coast up to the village. School boys on their way home from school had pelted the pastor's house with stones and injured Fatuatau's wife.

When she had finished treating the wound Sue angrily marched up to the village and confronted the policeman and councillors. 'These boys must be thrashed. If you won't respect your pastor I will take him away. Who is going to beat these boys?' The policeman and the village men refused. There had been five boys involved. The men said to Sue, 'You thrash them'. Sue sent the Ikeaga boys to get sticks, which they did very willingly, and she gave each of the miscreants six hearty cuts on the back.

The time for leave had come and Sue went to New Zealand where her brother Frank and his wife and family and her sister Eve were living near Palmerston North. While there Sue took courses in book-keeping and woodwork. She ended her leave staying in Tasmania with Gwen Milne, who was almost ready to return to Papua.

Seeing that her friend was still sad lest she be moved from her beloved district, Gwen sang Sue a little Welsh song. It made Sue laugh heartily because it was a funeral song! The five young missionaries sailing to Papua on the *John Williams* had a very happy trip. As well as Sue, Becky and Gwen Milne, the passenger list included two young men starting on their careers as missionaries, Eric Ure and Richard Owen. Their first landfall in Papua was Kwato at the southeastern tip. The missionaries there persuaded the passengers to take a trip into beautiful Milne Bay to see the stations and plantations of the Kwato Mission. The *John Williams* almost sailed without the five young missionaries.

Gwen accompanied Sue to Kalaigoro to be her companion for a while. When they visited some of the villages, because she was still convalescing, Gwen had to be carried. When they returned to Kalaigoro, the men who had carried her said to Sue, 'Sinabada, will you please tell your friend, before she comes back, to do without food for two weeks?' Not all white women were featherweights like Sue!

P.D.C. had no hesitation in giving Sue permission to continue in the Saroa-Boku district. She was elated. She could put into operation her plan to move the station. While preparing to move from Kalaigoro to Saroa, two things happened which delighted her heart. First she baptised those Ikeaga boys and welcomed them into the church. Then she installed Mamata into the Ikeaga group of villages.

When she returned from leave, Sue was welcomed by the Watsons and their new assistant manager, Mr Nicholson, who finally became manager of the plantation and a lifelong friend of the missionaries. Sue often met Nicholson on the road as he was driving to and from Gabagaba. He would offer her a lift and tease her, saying it was like having the Duchess of York on board because in every village the people came out to give Sue an enthusiastic welcome.

Sue had invited deacons as well as pastors to attend the quarterly meetings at Gabagaba. A small man from one of the Ikeaga villages came wearing the usual 'g-string' type belt and an army hat. He sat in the meeting with his hat on his head. When asked to report on the Ikeaga villages this gentle elderly man stood up straight, took off his hat, put it carefully on the floor, and said; 'Not much to report from our villages. You see, it's like this, we never get a tummy full of the Gospel in our villages, only a mouthful when someone happens to be passing by'. He went on to beg for a teacher to live with them and teach them properly. 'Then we shall have something to report', he said.

The answer to the old man's request was Mamata. He was a quiet, small man but a preacher and a very good leader. The young men from Ikeaga had been conducting services in other villages before Mamata arrived but now they had a leader and they became a very strong evangelistic group. Mamata visited far and wide and his own tribe really came to life. One young man came to Sue and asked for a New Testament. He explained that even though he was not a church member he had been going out taking services. He said that sometimes when he told a Bible story or quoted a verse the people wanted to know if what he said was true. 'I want a Bible,' he said, 'so that I can show them where it is in the Bible. Then they will believe it'.

When interviewing the people Mamata had prepared for baptism, Sue loved to watch their faces as Mamata translated her questions. It was so important to be sure that they understood what baptism meant and as Mamata asked each one who Jesus Christ was, why he came, about his death and resurrection, their eyes just shone and they were so confident in their answers. Sue felt sure that they did understand what faith and baptism and discipleship meant. Mamata was simple and humble and respected by the people.

One day while visiting Saroa, Sue picked up what looked like a baby being carried on her sister's back. She was very tiny, covered in huge ulcers called yaws and all her teeth had gone black and looked as though they were missing. Sue found that her mother had run off with a married man and left the little girl with her grandmother. The child was starving and Sue insisted that the woman bring little Gori to Kalaigoro so that she could care for her. Her big sister, Gagare, carried her to Kalaigoro and stayed to care for her. Sue treated her sores and cleaned her up and the schoolgirls prepared nourishing food for her. If anyone approached her while she was eating she would scream like a little animal.

Staffing was gradually improving, Pastor Nou Aire from Pari (not Nou Airi from Gabagaba) was sent to the district and Sue placed him at Karekodobu, sending Pastor Simona and his wife to Kware, the neighbouring village. Discouragement faded and the church grew and became strong as Sue travelled through the villages, teaching the people from God's Word and encouraging the pastors to be faithful in their work.

The Saroa people were very happy to have the headstation moved to their village. The piece of land they had chosen as the station site was a hill close to the village called Garagoro, or Burial Hill. Before the people became Christians their custom was to put the bodies of the dead on platforms in the village. When only the bones were left they were carried up Garagoro and placed under a tree. Each family had a tree. When the men were going out to fight they went to the hill and took some of the bones of their ancestors and wore them suspended round their necks.

The Hill of Dry Bones was to become a place of New Life. Mr Clark, who had worked in the district till 1917, was asked by P.D.C. to look at the site. He still felt strongly that the head station should be further inland. When he arrived at Saroa a service was being held to dedicate a memorial stone to Pastor Verave of Saroa who had worked in the inland villages. Surprised to see so many inland people at the service he said, 'I think I was wrong. This will make a good station for inland as well as coastal people'. It was decided that Pastor Nou Airi and the Sinaugoro people would build the house.

The time had come to leave Kalaigoro. The last evening's prayers were being held on the back veranda of the house. Everything was packed ready to leave early in the morning. Prayers were just finished when there was a loud crack. The veranda collapsed. No-one was hurt and the people laughed and said, 'We have finished with this place. It lasted just long enough, didn't it!' That night the boys and girls slept in various houses in the village.

Next morning a cavalcade of people left Kalaigoro, sad to say goodbye to their friends who had cared for them so well. There were carriers with the missionary's belongings, the students and their wives and children and household goods, and the missionary and her schoolchildren. Each child carried a mat, a pillow, and a bundle of clothes. The girls took it in turn to carry little Gori.

At the road the Kokebagu truck was waiting for them. Sue and the young ones rode on the truck to Saroa, where a temporary house had been built for them. The house proved too small for Sue and all her boarders, so Pastor Veniale suggested that he and his family use that house and Sue move into the pastor's house which was much more roomy.

On Saturdays when the little girls were off playing, Sue bathed and fed Gori. One day she was talking to Keve Bune, the chief of the Sinaugoro villages. He said, 'Is she all right?' Sue said, 'Yes, but she still doesn't like me very much'. Gori snuggled up to Sue and said, 'Iba'. From then on her baby-talk name for Sue was 'Iba'.

When Sue first went to Saroa there was a drought. These droughts seemed to come about every ten years. People searched the bush for wild yams and other roots. They got a small supply of water by digging a hole in the creek bed and waiting for the water to seep into it, then filling a length of bamboo. Sue had a very small kitchen with an iron roof and a six-hundred gallon tank. This water had to be shared with her boarders for cooking.

Because of the drought there was a lot of sickness and many terrible tropical ulcers. Babies were brought for treatment, their buttocks eaten away by ulcers which spread so quickly. When two babies died Sue decided to go to Port Moresby to learn to give injections and get a supply of codliver oil. She went down to Gabagaba, and Nou Airi took her to Port Moresby in his canoe. Sister Morley of the L.M.S. taught her to give the bismuth injections which were the treatment for tropical ulcers. Dr Strong, the Government Chief Medical Officer, refused to give Sue codliver oil, so she bought a supply herself and went home ready to treat the tropical ulcers. They still took a long time to heal but dressing daily and weekly injections helped. Some of the people lost limbs through neglecting tropical ulcers. The injections were very painful. Sue hated giving them, but it was before the days of penicillin or sulpha drugs. Gori was one of her first patients and became a happy, pretty little girl as her sores cleared up.

Gari from Kwalimurubu, about three kilometres from Saroa on the road to the coast, brought his little girl, Pita, for treatment. She had a huge ulcer on her leg and the bone was exposed. She was very good but cleaning up the sore took a great deal of water. One day while Sue was treating her a girl came and said the tank was empty. Sue told the girls they would have to go down to the creek and dig a hole for water.

Next day when Gari brought his little girl he said to Sue, 'Where shall I put the water?' He showed her a bamboo. Sue brought a bucket and he filled the bucket with water. Gari must have been up very early, sitting beside the hole he had made in the creek-bed and pouring the water drop by drop into his bamboo. Every day until the sore was healed that father brought a bamboo full of water as his contribution to the medical work of the day. The ulcer healed so well that later the little girl could not tell where it had been.

Gari and his wife became very close friends of Sue. They became Christians, joining the small church in their village. Their son became a boarder at Saroa and later trained as a pastor. They were a real 'Darby and Joan' couple, and when she died Gari was heart-broken. He would come and watch Sue as she did the medical treatments late in the afternoon. When the last patient had gone, Sue would have a chat and a prayer with him and off he would go.

Mr Chance, the government officer stationed at Rigo, was concerned about the people's health but he had no medical help. He had asked that a hospital be established at Rigo. In the meantime he arranged with Sue that he would bring the bad cases of ulcers and yaws he found on his patrols to the Government Station, accommodate them there and sent them every second day to Saroa for treatment.

When Sue arrived with all her boarders the school at Saroa became much larger. She helped Veniale supervise the school and prepared her student pastors for entrance to college as well as doing the medical work.

The young Tokelau Island pastor, Veniale, and his wife Lesia and children were to go to Port Moresby for a year where Veniale was to do a course in teacher training with Percy Chatterton. Sue was planning a quick inland patrol before Veniale left for Port Moresby. As she was leaving Lesia showed her a few small sores and asked for a bismuth injection. Sue had only a small supply of bismuth left and needed it for the inland villages. She asked Lesia to wait and see Sister Morley when she reached Port Moresby.

On the last day of her patrol Sue left Ikeaga at 4 a.m., accompanied by the young men acting as her carriers. They arrived at Kokebagu at 5 p.m., hoping to spend the night before returning to Saroa. A letter awaited them to say that Lesia had died that day and had been buried according to Sue's instructions that all bodies must be buried within twenty-four hours. Waiting only to drink a cup of tea, they then set off for Saroakei, where they found carriers to take over from the young Ikeaga men and continued on to Saroa arriving at midnight.

Next morning Sue heard the tragic tale. Some Papuan orderlies had arrived on patrol to give injections and Lesia had gone to have an injection. It was a new drug, said to be better than bismuth. She had the first injection and that night became violently ill and died before morning. Sue reported the matter to Port Moresby at once and the drug was withdrawn from use. Instead of going to Port Moresby for teacher training, the young pastor was sent home to Tokelau Island with his two small children.

A few years later the arrival of sulpha drugs, the first antibiotics, revolutionised the treatment of many infections. When one of the mission sisters from Port Moresby brought Sue the drugs, a man in a nearby village was very ill with pneumonia. Treated with sulphas, he made a good recovery and lived many more years.

Simona became headstation pastor at Saroa. Nou Airi and Simona were friends of long standing. Faauma his wife was willing to do anything. She taught the students' wives and girls from the village, sewing and mat-making. She led the village women and was invaluable when midwifery cases came along. When Sue went down with dysentery, Faauma took charge of her.

The work of building the house at Saroa was now getting under way. While those working on preparing the timbers went off to Karekodobu the men of the six Sinaugoro villages gave two days each in turn to level the hilltop. They took ten feet of earth off and used it to build up the sides of the hill to make the area larger. There was one large stone the men could not shift. Some of the old men from the village came. They looked at the rock and blew on it and smoothed it. They said, 'There's a way into everything if you can find it. There must be a little crack in here somewhere'. But they couldn't find it and eventually the house posts were placed round the rock.

Bob Rankin, who had been a draughtsman before going to theological college, had been given the job of drawing up the plans for the house. That meant quite a few letters between Bob and Sue as Sue explained her ideas for the design. Bob later said, 'There are more ways than one of throwing your hat in!'

Sue kept hearing stories of new colleagues on their arrival in Papua receiving a letter from Bob, telling them that their work would be much more effective if they were married. He also enlisted Mrs Turner's help in persuading Sue to marry him!

Meanwhile Sue was absorbed in preparations for the building. A cutting list for timber was made up by Mr Munroe, a builder who was a deacon of the Ela Church in Port Moresby. He trained many of the pastors in carpentry. The people of the villages were bringing gea, a hardwood, for the stumps for the house. Sue gave them the measurements she wanted and paid five shillings a post.

One day Mr Watson of Kokebagu asked Sue if she knew how to square a house. She had no idea at all, so Watson went to Saroa and squared the house and taught Sue how to use Pythagoras' theorem, 'square on the hypotenuse is equal to the sum of the squares on the other two sides', to plant the posts of a house at rightangles. At last she saw that geometry had some practical use. Sue was able to square a building herself. The Saroa, Gabagaba and Karekodobu people pitsawed timber. Mobaea, a whitish timber, the hardest available, was used for the inside studs.

Some people brought bundles of bamboo, about six sticks twelve to fourteen feet long. Sue paid a pound (500 grams) of rice for each six sticks. As the work went on those who brought in materials were paid and given a meal. There was a drought and everyone was hungry. The people said that the building of the mission house saved them from starvation. Faauma and the village girls did the cooking each day for the workers.

The older people sat under a tree near the pastor's house and cleaned and split and wove the bamboo into sheets which were then put out in the sun to dry. The sheets were used for lining the rooms and making shutters. This kept the older generation busy for weeks and provided with food.

The story goes that the people learned to weave bamboo from a Chinese man who was living at Rigo. One day when Mr Schlencker was living at Kalaigoro he went down to the Government Station at Rigo and met a Chinese man who was building a house for himself. The windows and doors were made of woven bamboo. So he said, 'When you have finished here would you like to come to Kalaigoro and do some work for me?' He taught the school boys and students to weave bamboo. There was plenty of bamboo inland, so everywhere the boys and students went they taught their new skill. If missionaries found a village where the people knew how to weave bamboo, they knew a pastor had once worked in that village.

Sue had set herself a heavy program. School was held three days a week — Mondays, Tuesdays and Thursdays. She helped in the school when she could. She ordered the food supplies. As well as feeding the people working at Saroa, supplies of rice, meat and tobacco had to be sent to the pitsawing groups. On Sunday nights she gave the men their cutting lists of timber needed for the coming week. One Thursday afternoon she would walk to Karekodobu to check the timber that had been cut and the next week on Friday walk to Gabagaba to check on the timber being pitsawn there. She always came home with a gift of fish from Gabagaba which the boarders shared. Sue enjoyed those hours on the bush tracks; she got to know her companions very well as they chatted about many things.

Mr English, the trader from Rigo, brought the timber from Saroakei to Saroa. One day he shouted at Sue; 'How are you managing it? You are getting the best timber in the country and I don't agree with it!'

Everything except the roofing iron and the tongued-and-grooved timber for the floors was made locally. Mr Clark arranged for the flooring to come from Sydney.

Some people from down the Kemp Welch River came bringing timber for the house stumps. Sue asked them why they were helping when they belonged to the Hula District. They said they wanted to belong to Saroa. Sue talked to Mr Short and he agreed that if Sue could provide pastors for those villages, they should return to the care of the Saroa district. Among those who came to help were some young men from Tauruba. They explained that their fathers were unwilling to help, so they had come. When Sue talked to them she found that they were the boys she had beaten for ill-treating their pastor!

The land was levelled, the site for the house squared off and pegged out, the timber stacked on the site and the young men who had been doing the pitsawing arrived to start building. Nou Airi arrived to supervise.

Meanwhile a house for the boys was being built close by. When the floor was being put down Sue looked at it and said to Simona, 'Are you sure the floor is level? It doesn't look right to me'. It was very crooked so Sue helped to get it level. From that day if someone in the village was building a house they sent for Sue to check the levels. She got the reputation for having a straight eye. When all the buildings were finished there was accommodation for four student families, twenty boys and the girls boarders who lived in Sue's house.

Sue very quickly adapted to Papuan ways and understood their thought processes but she still knew that she needed to control her hot temper. When the timber was being cut one person consistently cut his timber short. Nou Airi was very patient about it but one day Sue became angry and had her say to Timo. A man whom Sue did not know was standing beside Timo. He said, 'She's angry'. Timo turned to the man, pointed to his mouth, smiled and motioned 'yes'. Then he pointed to his chest and motioned 'no'. Sue suddenly remembered that the people were afraid of the power of anger, and often blamed it for illness or death. The wise old pastor was explaining to the stranger that Sue was angry in word but not in her heart. The man was satisfied.

The house went up till one day Sue was in school when a group of workers invited her to go up to the top of the hill. The roof was on, the floor laid and the steps were in place. A great cheer went up as Sue climbed the steps into the house.

When the bamboo walls and shutters were completed and the cleaning up finished, a feast was held. All the workers sat down in the house and were served by the rest of the people and then the others had their feast in the open air.

The builders insisted that God must have really wanted that house built because there was not one accident during the building. The mood of happiness and praise to God at that feast assured Sue that she was accepted into the community.

She had a home with a front veranda, a back veranda, and a row of rooms between. There was her own bedroom, a dining room, a visitor's room, the girls' room and a kitchen. At the end of the veranda was a spot Sue walled off to use as an office. Tanks were ordered to give a water supply, and Sue and Vaita stained the floors brown. Under the house was room for a tool store, workshop and classroom. Later a store was built at the foot of the hill with room for a vehicle underneath. After that, the supplies were brought up from Gabagaba by truck and the quarterly meetings held at Saroa. This house is still in use by the circuit minister at Saroa.

Chapter 6

Sorcery? Spirits?

The number of people lining up on the back veranda of the mission house each afternoon for medical treatment was growing. Sue worked till dark treating yaws, malaria, injuries, tropical ulcers and many other complaints.

About half the people of Saroa suffered from a skin disease they called 'sipoma'. It was a type of tinea which spread in dry scaly whorls all over the body, and looked very unattractive. The Health Department issued a paint which was made up of methylated spirits, salicylic acid and other things including a green dye. Only a small area of the body could be treated at a time. It was a painful treatment and it was not easy to persuade the people to submit to it. One of the students' wives was the first person Sue prevailed upon to be transformed.

Then starting work on the boys of the village she said, 'You won't get a nice-looking wife if you have this ugly skin disease'. The boys came to be treated. Then she used the same persuasion on the girls although she knew that in most cases a marriage had already been arranged!

It was all very time-consuming. Then one of the student pastors came to Sue; 'We have been having a meeting. We think you are working too hard. Perhaps we could help with some of the medicines. We could paint the people with sipoma and give out codliver oil. Maybe we could clean up some of the sores'. From then on two students and two boys were rostered to help with the medicines each day.

The missionaries' medicine was often resorted to only when sorcery had failed. On hearing the noise of a crowd of people passing by, Sue looked out of the classroom window. A man was being carried along the road. She ran out to ask what had happened. 'He has been bitten by a snake and we are taking him home to Kwalimurubu', was the answer. Sue's offers of help were refused and the procession went on its way. About seven that evening, someone came to ask Sue to go to the man. Timo, the Kwalimurubu pastor, came too. He said, 'Don't go. The sorcerer has had his turn and failed. There is nothing you can do now. The sorcerer has told them to send for you. If you go he will say that you interfered and that if you had not he could have saved the man'. Sue trusted Timo and took his advice. Snakebite was very common and the people feared snakes greatly because they believed that a spirit or sorcerer had caused the snake to bite the person.

During a whooping cough epidemic there was a constant stream of people coming to the house for cough mixture. The medicine was mixed by Sue from ingredients supplied by the Health Department. The demand was so great that very soon the bottles were empty. One of the students' wives told Sue of a very effective cough medicine made from leaves.

Grasping at a solution to her problem Sue said, 'Bring me lots of the leaves'. She and the students' wives washed them and boiled them. They tasted terrible so Sue added honey and lime juice. She dosed her patients with this concoction and when the honey ran out flavoured it with golden syrup.

One day Sue saw Pastor Timo walking up the hill. He seemed to have a problem. Every now and then he would double up. When he reached the steps Sue saw that he was laughing so much he could scarcely walk. 'This medicine you're using,' he gasped, 'it's not for coughs'. 'What is it used for?' asked Sue, concerned. 'If a woman has too many children of one sex we give her lots of that medicine so that the next baby will be of the opposite sex!' Sue chuckled, 'Don't you tell the people what I've been using,' she warned Timo, 'Remember, my medicine is different because it had lime juice and honey in it'.

After school each afternoon Sue would attempt to take a solitary walk in the quiet of the bush. But the children followed her, shouting and banging the trees with sticks. At last Sue turned to them and said, 'Why are you making such a noise? I would like to walk by myself'. The children answered, 'We couldn't let you do that.

Don't you know that the spirits are everywhere and if you are alone they will hurt you? We go with you and make plenty of noise to let them know there are lots of people coming so they won't harm you'.

Sue had much to learn. There were spirits of the bush, the hills, the streams and rivers and rocks. Most of them were angry and spiteful. There were also the sorcerers in each village who harnessed the power of evil to cause illness and death. Then there were the 'vada'. Were they spirits or humans?

Appeasing the spirits was very important to ensure the fertility of the gardens and success in hunting. When the Saroa people loaned Sue a piece of land to use as a garden for food for her boarders, everyone in the village turned out to help clear the land. Before cutting down the trees they had a hymn, a Bible reading and a prayer. They told Sue that most villages still observed the old fertility rites, but since they had become Christians they now prayed before making a garden.

When all the debris was dry enough to burn, the people returned to the garden to burn off and place the big logs in rows across the steep hillside. This prevented erosion when tropical downpours sent torrents of water gushing down the slope. After planting banana suckers, yams, sweet potatoes, maniota, taro, pawpaw trees and a few clumps of sugarcane, the women sat down with Sue to have a rest. They started explaining their old customs.

They said that when they planted sweet potatoes and yams they always put certain leaves under them. They asked Sue if this was wrong. She replied that she did not know, but in her country when they planted potatoes the farmers always dug a trench and put manure in it, put the potatoes in and covered them with soil. They continued, 'We used to name the names of all the spirits over the things we planted. Was that wrong?' Sue said, 'I don't know, tell me about that custom'. 'When a family chose a site for a new garden,' the women explained, 'before any work was done, the oldest man in the family was sent to the piece of land with a coconut leaf basket. He carried it in front of him suspended from his shoulders. The basket was filled with small chunks of sugarcane. Walking all over the land to be cleared he broadcast the sugarcane, naming the spirits of his family. Only after he had returned to the village did the men go out with their bush knives to start the work of clearing'.

The women described how the men of Gidobada, the heathen village a kilometre from Saroa, prepared for hunting. The old men placed all the spears, nets, clubs and other equipment in a heap and one man would name the names of the spirits over them. Then they would take up their weapons and go off to the hunt. If some made a kill and one man did not catch anything he would ask his spirits why they weren't helping him as the other men's ancestral spirits

55

were helping them. 'What's the matter with you?' he would scold. After that he would probably catch something.

Sue tells in her own words the story of the children and the sugarcane:

From Kalaigoro I was going with my school children on a visit to some villages. There were about six girls and ten or twelve boys. We were walking single file through the bush. At one of the villages they had given us some sugarcane. We each had a nice chunk. I was chewing mine to suck the sweet juice out and then throwing the pith away. Then I realised that I had walked ahead and the girls were quite a way back, so I waited for them. When they came up their hands were full of my chewed sugarcane pith. They explained that they were slow because they had picked up every piece that I had thrown away. I asked why.

They said, 'If someone who doesn't like you finds it, he can take it to the sorcerer who will make medicine and you may get sick or die'. I called them all to me and said, 'Listen, I have come to tell you about Jesus Christ and he is stronger than all the sorcerers and he has promised to look after us. So we don't need to be afraid of sorcerers. There's nobody who can hurt us. Jesus is with us and he is looking after us all the time. I want you to try it. I want you to throw all this stuff away and you'll see, in about three week's time when we get home, nobody will have been sick and nobody will have died, because Jesus is looking after us'.

The children agreed, threw away the pith and on we went. We were away about three weeks, going from village to village, staying a couple of days in each. When we got home I heard them say, 'Well, it's true, nobody got sick and nobody has died, so it must be true, Jesus is strong, he does look after us'.

A different kind of spirit was a sort of bogey-man parents used to frighten their children called a 'koboni'.

On one patrol Sue and her party were sleeping in the pastor's house at Ikeaga. They were planning to leave at four a.m. and walk through to Kokebagu the next day. During the night someone seemed to be moving about so Sue called out, 'It's not time yet, go back to sleep'. There was silence for a short time and then rustling and clatter again. At four a.m. Sue woke everyone, they had a short prayer and set off. At breakfast time, as they rested on the banks of a stream and cooked their food, Sue remarked that someone had been very restless during the night. She asked if anything had been wrong.

The men all looked at one another and said that no-one had been moving about. After a silence one man said, 'It must have been the koboni'. 'What koboni?' asked Sue. They told her that a koboni inhabited that house. They reminded Sue how the first time she and Miss Beckett had visited Ikeaga, Becky had sat on the floor while they were singing hymns. Then suddenly she jumped up and sat on the bench beside Sue because something was pinching her leg. That

56

was the koboni. Sue was sure something had been moving around in the house during the night!

Koboni were not bad spirits, but mischievous sprites like Puck in *A Midsummer Night's Dream*. But what of 'vada'? Often when the missionaries asked why someone had died unexpectedly, they were told, 'Vada did it'. The people said that these beings, dressed up in grass and leaves, would waylay the person they wanted to kill, tell him that on a certain day he was going to die, and then tap him on the back of the head just hard enough to knock him out. When he regained consciousness the man would be very frightened and on the day named he would die.

The people told Sue the story of a very brave chief, who not long before her arrival in the district resolved to settle the matter of whether 'vada' were human or not.

The chief's name was Kone and his village Babaga. One night when Kone and his younger brother were sleeping in the shack at their garden where they had been working the 'vada' started walking round outside the garden fence. They poked their heads over the fence but the brothers could only see bunches of leaves. Then the 'vada' started walking round the village at night. Each morning the village people were frightened at the strange footprints round the outside of the village fence.

At last the chief said, 'I'm going to find out who they are'. He took his younger brother with him and started following the tracks. They came to one of the Lagumi villages. The Lagumi people were feared for their strong sorcery. The two men talked to the Lagumi chief but when they left the village the old chief said to his brother, 'There's going to be trouble here. I won't get home alive, but you go as fast as you can to Rigo and report. Don't wait for me, I can't run'.

The younger brother ran on ahead but when he heard the 'vada' coming he climbed up a very leafy tree and watched. Sure enough, they caught up with the old man, spoke to him and clubbed him, but he was too old and he died immediately instead of merely being knocked out. When the 'vada' saw he was dead they lost their heads and slashed his face. His brother was too frightened to move. He stayed in the tree till dark, then ran all the way to Rigo. He told Mr Vivian who called out his police and by morning had the village surrounded. The 'vada' were arrested and spent many years in jail.

In spite of the bravery of the old chief, fear of 'vada' still continued. In 1946 Sue wrote;

There is still much talk about 'vada'. Inland the people are very frightened. When we ask them why some villages are getting smaller they say that 'Vada' killed them. We have found only two young men who appear to be free of such beliefs. Both have been medical orderlies and are sons of teachers and brought up on the mission station. Such men will be able to do far more for their people than we can ever hope to do.

The Spirit of God was breaking through. Sue recounted an incident:

The older school children had spent a day of Bible study and celebration with me in one of the Sinaugoro villages. I was to stay the night in the village. As the tropical night descended, the young people went off into the darkness singing and shouting happily. They had about eight kilometres to walk to their own villages. I asked the pastor, 'Aren't they afraid?' 'No, not now,' he replied, 'While they believe in Jesus and follow him they are not afraid, but if ever they leave him the old fears will all come back'.

In the L.M.S. magazine *The Chronicle*, May 1964, Sue summarised what she had learnt of the religion of Papua and its relationship to Christianity:

Fear is the essence of animism, and the work of keeping the people safe from the anger of the spirits engages much time and talent. Even our pastors admit that they are still burdered with (fear). Animism is a way of explaining evil and calamity. Somebody is angry. Who? Will he withdraw his anger? What can I give to bring about this reconciliation?

To Papuans, life is one. There is no dividing between sacred and secular. Human beings, spirits and inanimate things are all bound up together. Religion has to do with every event of everyday life. In this, at least the Scriptures seem to agree.

So often men who have powers of sorcery or even of 'vada' are keen to become church members, and are willing to give up their power of hurting people and of talking with the spirits. But our young pastors say that the complete renunciation of these powers is very rare. If a trained sorcerer gave up his power he would be at the mercy of other sorcerers. So he must hold on to some residue of power as a personal safeguard. Along with this incomplete renunciation, such people may present the superficial appearance of enthusiastic Christians.

Where then can Christianity break through? Our word now used for prayer is 'guriguri' which was the word used for calling in the spirits to help. Our word for holy is 'helaga', the word used for a man who fasted for some special purpose (to become a sorcerer or have special powers in hunting, for example).

Some parts of the Bible are more easily understood by Papuans than by us. The vocabulary of the Old Testament often meets the demands of communication surprisingly well. They know so much about peace-offerings and propitiation between people and people and between people and spirits. They understand blood-offerings although I doubt whether they really understand the first thing about redemption in our sense. The idea of 'first-fruits' is also not strange to them. Prayer, the presence of the Holy Spirit and the love of God are things they have certainly come to understand.

Nou Airi

One who showed a deep understanding of the Gospel truths was Pastor Nou Airi of Gabagaba. He worked faithfully, and church membership was growing.

Sue appreciated more and more what a remarkable and saintly man he was. Remembering Mr Short's remarks when she had first met Nou Airi, Sue asked him, 'Nou, how did you become a Christian and a pastor?' He told her this story:

Like Jacob of Old Testament times I made a bargain with God.

When I was a young boy I was taught to read and write by a Nieuean pastor in my village Gabagaba. As a teenager I began work as a pilot on the Governor's yacht, *The Merrie England*. I loved the work and was told that I was a good pilot.

Soon after I started work I married a very good girl. But often when I came home from a trip I gave her a beating. Why? It was the custom. Perhaps it was to make sure she behaved herself while I was away. One Saturday afternoon I arrived home and as usual started to thrash my wife. Once I started I could not stop. Suddenly I realised she was not moving. I looked at her lying there on the floor and thought I had killed her. My first thoughts were for myself. If she were dead her relatives would kill me.

I ran off into the jungle in terror, on and on till it was too dark to see. Full of grief I sat down on the roots of a tree. I did love my wife. There were evil spirits all around me. I tried to sleep but I was terrified of the spirits and very sorry for what I had done.

Then I remembered the words of that Niuean pastor, 'Jehovah God is always near us. He listens to our prayers and answers them'. I stood up and folded my arms as I had been taught to do when praying and said aloud, 'I've heard about you, that you listen to prayer and answer it. Well, I'm praying to you now. I want to go back in the morning and find my wife alive. If I do I promise that I'll serve you all my life'.

I lay down and went peacefully to sleep. When I woke at first light and remembered, I went weak with fear. I wanted to run away. But I thought of my prayer and said to myself, 'I must keep my bargain'.

As I started to push my way through the bush towards the track, I heard footsteps and again I wanted to turn and run. I fearfully stood my ground on the track till in the dawn light I could see that it was my wife coming towards me! How glad I was to see her! We sat on a rock by the track and talked and talked. I told her of my bargain with God. 'I promised to serve God all my life if I went back to the village and found you alive'. 'All right', she replied, 'I will follow God, too'. Hand in hand we went back to the village to tell the pastor that we wanted to join the Seekers' Class to learn how to become Christians.

I continued to work on *The Merrie England* but I was not very satisfied. I said to my wife, 'When I promised to serve God all my life did I mean working on the boat, attending church when I'm home, saying my prayers and reading my Bible, or did I mean something more?' My wife said, 'Let's go and talk to the pastor'.

The pastor suggested that I train to become a pastor. I spent four years at Vatorata with Dr Lawes and was then sent to work in one of the inland villages.

That was more than twenty years ago, concluded Nou Airi.

When Sue came to live in the district Nou Airi was still refusing to submit to the old heathen ways. Every few years the villages held a big feast with dancing called a 'gaba'. The gaba was the name of the drum used in the dancing. Many gardens were planted to provide food for the feast and the leader of the dance visited the other villages to invite the people to take part and help supply garden food and pigs. Gifts of food, grass skirts, spears and coconuts were prepared. They were all offered to the spirits by putting them on the spirit platform and naming the names of the ancestral spirits over them. The gifts were then distributed among the guests.

The men danced to the beat of the drums. A few women and girls danced on the edge of the crowd with much swaying of grass skirts and an inviting flicker of buttocks and thighs. The married women watched jealously from the sidelines. If a man touched one of the girls his wife would explode into shrill abuse and violence. The dances were always characterised by promiscuity and domestic brawls.

The Christians did not take part in these feasts but one year the dance leader in Gabagaba decided that he was going to persuade Nou Airi to go back to heathenism. He invited Nou to the dance and feast. Nou was aware of what was happening but it would have caused offence to the village people to refuse. He called the Christians together and said; 'Unless you are very sure that you can stand firm, don't have anything to do with the dance. Go into my house with your wives and pray for the rest of us'.

Most of the Christians went into the pastor's house and Nou Airi and some of the other strong Christians went to the feast. There were plenty of presents. They offered gifts to Nou Airi and he refused them. They even offered him a pig and he said, 'Look, I can take these things that you are offering me but I would still be a Christian. Nothing you can give me would make me change my mind. I won't go back'. They became angry and threatened him with spears but he still stood firm. The visitors from the other villages said, 'We would never treat a pastor like that in our villages'.

60

Then they walked off in disgust. So the dance finished and not one of the Christians went back to the heathen practices.

A few weeks later Sue was in school and the leader of the dance in Gabagaba came up and sat beside her on a bench and said, 'You know, Mother, that we had a big feast and dance at Gabagaba?' She said, 'Yes, I heard'. He said, 'You know that we tried hard to get Nou Airi to come back to our way?' She said, 'Yes, I heard'. He said simply, 'We didn't get him but he got me. I've come to tell you that I want to join the Seekers' Class'. That was the end of the heathen feasts in Gabagaba and the beginning of the growth of the church.

Sue was very content. Her life was full and satisfying. She was seeing people set free from darkness and death.

Chapter 7

Leaving Saroa?

Each Wednesday evening a service was held in the village street at Saroa. As Sue led the procession of school boys and girls carrying hurricane lamps winding down the track from the mission station on the hilltop, she was very happy. She reflected on the satisfying life she led, no time for being bored or lonely.

But changes were coming. Sue had told the Lord that she was willing to marry Robert Rankin even if it meant leaving the people she loved so much. The pastors had said to Sue, 'Now we are all getting used to each other we think the L.M.S. will take you away and send you to another district as it did Mr Short'.

Now after two years living at Saroa, Sue had to break the news that she would be getting married. She told the pastors and they listened very quietly and then went away. Then two came back and said, 'We have just had a little committee and we want to ask you some questions'. Sue agreed and the questions were put. 'Will you lose those letters that you have before and after your name?' Sue explained that they would not change. 'Will you have to stop preaching?' Sue replied that she would be doing the same work, but she and her husband would be able to serve the Lord better as a team.

The two men went away to report to their fellow pastors and came back, saying, 'In that case we agree to you getting married but we are going to send a deputation to Committee to ask that you both come back here'. Sue gently suggested that if the Lord wanted her back at Saroa he would arrange it. They agreed that that was a better way. Mary I of England had said that she would die with 'Calais' written on her heart and Sue was quite certain that 'Saroa' was indelibly printed on hers.

In a letter to a member of the L.M.S. board in London, dated 2 May 1931, Sue wrote;

I am glad to know that you are deciding to look for a man to succeed me at Saroa. I really think that it's too big a job for a woman, for the walking is endless and the climbing terrific. From the point of view of the friendliness of the people it couldn't be better, but it does not lessen the difficulties. I fortunately am used to the hills and, in the bargain, am lighter in weight than a jockey, so that people find no difficulty in carrying me up the hills, but even I find it hard going at times, and I think I would be wrong to urge you to put another woman in my place.

But I hope you will find a successor very soon for those people have been such bricks in the preparation of the new house and now, far from being angry with me for letting them down, are working overtime at the building so that I will have the pleasure of living in the house before I leave. They are quite the most loyal and encouraging people I have met, and leaving them is going to be very hard.

As a matter of fact they are asking to have Robert Rankin here but I don't think that is a likely solution and Saroa would be much more encouraging for a new man than Moru — though needless to say, I'd love to stay on here.

When Tom Bowes heard that Sue was to be married, he invited her to Gobaragere plantation for tea. The silver tea service was not in evidence, and Sue remarked on the fact. 'I gave it away', he said as he poured tea from an earthenware pot. As Sue took her leave he handed her a parcel containing the silver tea service. It was Bowes' wedding gift to her.

Bob and Sue were to be married at Delena in November 1931 by R. L. Turner. But first they attended P.D.C., where they were the attendants at Gwen Milne's and Eric Ure's marriage. Becky and Richard Owen were also among the six couples married during 1931.

Because of the number of weddings, there was a great deal of discussion at Committee about placing staff. When they married, the young women were 'demoted' from missionary to missionary's wife. This change of status for Sue is reflected in the official records of the L.M.S. Sue's first period of service in Papua is recorded as lasting from 1925 to 1931! The many years of leadership she was to give after her marriage are ignored.

To Sue's joy, Bob was appointed district missionary of the Saroa Boku district. Committee asked that after their wedding at Delena, they proceed to Moru and prepare to hand over the district to another missionary before going to Saroa.

At Delena, Mrs Turner welcomed the bride and bridegroom. She was delighted that her prayers were being answered and had prepared with great care for the celebration. Gwen and Eric Ure were the attendants. Mrs Turner had even taught the school children a Welsh song but Sue says Bob whisked her away so quickly onto that canoe for Moru that she does not remember hearing it!

The new bride found that she had a husband with a very dry sense of humour. He told her that since they were married on Armistice Day — 11 November — he could at least be assured of two minutes' silence a year! He teased Sue, saying that she had married him so that she could remain five years longer in the country, since men retired five years later than women.

Bob had been missionary at Moru for four years and had found it a very lonely station. Now he brought a bride, three of her school girls from Saroa, and little Gori whom Sue had adopted. The overnight trip from Delena was a new experience for the little girls from Saroa. There was no sheltered anchorage at Moru and the Delena men navigated the canoe skilfully through the surf and far up on to the beach.

Beyond the beach stood the roomy old mission house with its thatched roof. It was infested with fleas. Sue's first chore, with the help of the Samoan pastor's wife, was to put all the bedding out in the sun and wash the walls and floors with kerosene.

The normal routines of the mission station took over for both Sue and Bob. The Turners and Owens came to stay. The South Sea pastors and their wives were holding their annual meetings or 'fono' in a nearby village. Sue went down with 'flu but quickly recovered. The Owens went on to their posting at Orokolo and the Turners returned to Delena. Then disaster struck. The 'flu epidemic spread to the South Sea people.

One pastor died and the entire group moved into the Samoan guest house to be cared for. The only drugs the missionaries had were quinine and aspirin, but they did their best to care for the patients. One man was very ill, started to recover, and went to sleep in the school on the cement floor. He developed pneumonia and there was little Sue could do for him.

Within a few weeks there were five fresh graves on the hill near the mission house. There had been no new cases for a while when suddenly Bob became very ill. There were many South Sea patients who still needed constant care. Making a quick decision, Sue asked the station pastor to borrow two canoes. She would take Bob and an Ellice Island couple who were still very ill to Mrs Turner at Delena. Mrs Turner was a trained nurse and would know how to care for them.

Having sailed through the night to reach Delena, Sue left her patients in Mrs Turner's care, confident that they would receive the treatment they needed. She received some criticism for leaving her husband when he was so ill. Her reply was; 'I knew Bob was in good hands, but the people at Moru had no-one to care for them'.

Another Samoan woman died. Sue felt that fear played a large part in her death.

Bob was soon back at Moru, and the Ellice Islands couple were recovering at Delena. On Christmas Day Mrs Turner allowed them to have dinner with another South Sea family. The Ellice Island man collapsed and died. Soon after that, his wife lost all will to live. Their one-year-old girl was adopted by Pastor Simona of Saroa, who came to Delena and took her home.

A cutting from the *Sydney Morning Herald* of 13 February 1932 expressed the tragedy of the situation, which had caused seven bereaved adults, and thirteen children who had lost parents, to be waiting in Sydney for passage to their island homes.

While Sue was nursing her patients, little Gori played happily on the veranda. Each time she saw Sue she would say to herself, 'Gori, get out of the way', all Sue had time to say to the little girl for weeks.

The time came for the Rankins to load their possessions on a boat bound for Gabagaba. There they hired a trader's truck to take them to Saroa. Just as they came to the foot of the hills, near Gomore, the truck broke down. Their goods were stacked into an empty house in Gomore and Sue, Bob, Gori and the three girls walked up the road to Saroa.

The 'flu epidemic had hit Saroa as well but half the people turned out to give Sue and her husband a welcome that amazed Bob. Having escorted them up the hill to the house they said; 'Now, where are your goods?' Without hesitation they set off, men and women, to carry the things to Saroa. Time after time they made the trip of nine kilometres down the hills and nine kilometres back till everything that had been left at Gomore was safely in the missionaries' house. Now Bob knew why Sue felt she had come home.

To Bob and Sue, a son

It was six years since Sue had arrived in Papua, and time for her to take a year's leave in Great Britain. She and Bob were delighted that she was expecting a child, but a bout of boils and her recent experiences at Moru had left her very tired and thin. Bob was due for short leave in Australia. Soon after the couple had settled in to their first home together at Saroa, they sailed on the *Macdhui* for Sydney. Sue hoped to spend a short leave in Melbourne with Bob and then return with him to Papua, but the doctor and mission board insisted that she take her year's leave with her family in Wales. Bob returned to Saroa alone.

The sea voyage to England was almost the end of Sue. She was very ill. The stewardess and Mrs Eastman, a missionary from the Gilbert Islands, nursed her, keeping her alive. When Sue's sisters, Margaret and Blodwen, met her at the docks she weighed thirty-five kilos and was brought off the ship in a wheelchair, too weak to walk. The members of the mission board wanted her to enter a nursing home in London, thinking that she would not live long. Sue pleaded to be allowed to go home to her brother, Tom. 'When I get home I'll be all right'.

Tom met her at the junction where she changed trains to go to Llanfyllin. Both Tom and the old guard who had known her as a child, tried to hide their tears from Sue as they lifted her into the carriage.

The townspeople were horrified to see their beloved missionary daughter so weak and thin. The doctor asked Tom to convince Sue that she would not return to Papua. She knew that her illness was not only due to pregnancy and began to suspect that she had a tumour. But she refused to believe that she would never return to Papua. Sue knew that her work there had only just begun and that she would be returning to her husband and her people.

Robert Ellis Rankin was born in Liverpool in January 1933. Sue, by sheer coincidence, was in the Robert Rankin Ward of the hospital. All went well with the birth. After a few days with friends in Liverpool, an old schoolmaster friend took Sue and the baby back to her brother's farm. Bob and his little cousin spent hours in their prams outside the farmhouse door in the sun. One of Tom's sheep dogs appointed himself their guardian and refused to leave the children to do his usual duties.

From the window Sue would watch the dog licking the babies' faces and both children laughing. Although she regained a little strength and could take the baby for short walks in his pram, Sue knew that she was not recovering as she should. She felt very weak and could not keep food down. One leg kept getting stiff. The doctor at Shrewsbury assured her that she was quite healthy.

When baby Bob was seven-months-old, Sue went to London for a medical examination in preparation for her return to Papua. The L.M.S. doctor, Dr Basil Price, was surprised that she was still not well. 'I think I have a tumour', she told him. After the examination, he confirmed that there was a growth in the bowel and sent her back to the doctor in Liverpool who had cared for her during her confinement. He agreed with the diagnosis. At last Sue knew that there was a reason for her weakness and discomfort.

Although the two doctors agreed that the tumour was probably malignant, they suggested that Sue return to Australia rather than spend another winter in Britain. They felt that her illness was very serious. The mission board arranged a passage on a one-class ship back to Melbourne, where she would receive treatment. Many of the fellow passengers were very kind, caring for the baby each afternoon while Sue rested.

Bob was waiting in Melbourne to meet his wife and hold in his arms his infant son. Sue's sister, Eve, was also in Melbourne, having just arrived from New Zealand. Eve was a children's nurse and was working for a Welsh family who were settling in Melbourne.

The doctors in Melbourne acted quickly and within a few days Eve was caring for the baby while Sue was in hospital for surgery. Three weeks later Sue was discharged, already feeling much stronger. Bob told her that the Saroa people were praying for her and had no doubt that she would return to them.

When Sue was feeling a little better, Bob returned to Papua while Sue waited impatiently to be released by the doctors to follow him. Finally they gave way to Sue's pleading although they felt that she had only about six months to live, but did not tell her of their prognosis. On her first shopping trip after her illness, Sue went to the L.M.S. office in the city. When she heard the news that she was free to return to Papua Sue tossed her new hat to the ceiling. In spite of knowing the doctors' verdict, the office staff could not help laughing at her joy, and set about booking her passage for her.

Eve accompanied Sue and the baby, now sixteen-months-old, on the m.v. *Van Rees*. Bob, and Gwen Ure, Sue's closest friend, welcomed them at Port Moresby wharf. What a reunion! The first little Papuan boy the toddler saw was a lad from Daru named Sammy. Little Bob seemed very puzzled at the colour of Sammy's skin. Very soon they became the best of friends.

Sue, Bob, Eve and the baby were at the wharf bright and early a few days later to leave for Gabagaba. The boat was late leaving and then Eve was very sick during the rough trip. At Gabagaba they had to wait for the trader's truck that Bob had booked to take them to Saroa. The Gabagaba people took them from the boat to the pastor's house, where they were welcomed with a meal.

As darkness was closing in they reached Saroa. The people had been waiting all day. When they heard the truck they rushed along the village street, hurricane lamps swinging, to greet their missionaries at the lorry shed at the foot of the hill. The baby was eagerly taken and willing hands unloaded the truck while the travellers walked wearily up the hill. The house was glowing with flowers and Henry, the cook, had the kettle boiling and a meal ready.

As the village people happily retraced their steps down the hill,

Sue thought; 'I'm home again! There is no village in the whole of Papua that can equal Saroa for a welcome!'.

It was back to work for everyone. Sue still tired easily and when she became frustrated because she could not do much, she went down to the village and talked to the people. They encouraged her. Eve learnt Motu, helped with the store and did the medical work. She stayed two years and became a second mother to young Bob.

To Sue, Bob seemed very Scottish and dour. At times she could not understand his burr and at times it was to her advantage to pretend that she did not understand. After such a long separation it took a while for them to adjust to each other. Sue appreciated Bob's firmness in discipline because she knew that the people found it easy to twist her round their little fingers.

Bob did not like dealing with sores and the routine of afternoon sick parade, but would help Sue when necessary. But the people knew that in an emergency he would take a great deal of trouble. One afternoon he arrived at Saroa from an inland patrol to find that a woman had been bitten by a snake. The sorcerer had been called but had not been able to help her. Her throat was paralysed by the poison and Bob stayed with her, massaging her throat and trying to feed her with warm milk. After a few hours she regained consciousness and by morning she had recovered. The people were very impressed because it was rare for anyone to recover from snakebite. Snakebite was very common and the people feared snakes greatly because they believed that a spirit or sorcerer had caused the snake to bite the person. As this fear was overcome and people began to have confidence in God, many people did recover.

Bob was always looking for crops that could become cash crops for the local people. Just before World War II broke out in the Pacific he organised planting of rice at Iogobada on the Kemp Welch River. The pastor and the student pastors cleared a large piece of land and then the students' wives and station children joined them at Iogobada for a week's picnic to plant rice. Everyone stood in a straight line, made a hole in front of each foot with a piece of stick and dropped a couple of rice seeds in each hole. Then they took one step forward and repeated the process till the area was covered. The resulting crop was very good and Bob waited for the opportunity to encourage the commercial growing of rice.

Bob also felt that peanuts could be a cash crop and a source of protein for the village people. On the flat land below the mission house he and Sue had a garden made for the children of each village that attended the Saroa school, and one for the station children, six plots in all. Peanuts were planted and a good crop resulted. When they were harvested Sue and Bob asked the children to take the nuts home and ask their parents to plant them in their gardens. When they later asked the parents how the peanuts were growing they did not know anything about them. All the nuts had been eaten on the way home from school! Later, peanuts were grown commercially at Rigo and on a plantation on the Kemp Welch River.

Chapter 8

The pastors and people

Timo Tanu told Sue that he became a pastor because of his friend Nou Airi. When he was a school boy at Vatorata his job was to look after Mrs Lawes' chickens. Later he was promoted to the kitchen and after Dr and Mrs Lawes left and before Mrs turner arrived, he was cook to the Rev. R. L. Turner.

Nou Airi, already working as a pastor, said, 'You ought to be a teacher, too, but you are too fond of a full tummy and afraid of being hungry!' Timo thought it over and decided that perhaps it was true, left his job as cook and went into the college as a student.

After training, his first charge was Kware on the Kemp Welch River. The Rev. Percy Schlencker lived at Kalaigoro and had just opened up that area. But Timo was not strong. He had suffered much from rheumatism and fever since childhood.

Sue first experienced Timo's leadership when he was pastor of Kwalimurubu in the incident of the cricket game. When a row flared between the Saroa and Kwalimurubu teams, he threatened to take his men home and withdraw from helping to build the house unless the rules were kept. After the mission house was built came a second experience. Sue had written a letter to the pastor-teachers and wanted to address them as 'my colleagues'. She finally headed it, 'You who work together with me'. That afternoon Timo came to the house with the letter in his hand. 'Why did you say this?' he

Sue Ellis on her graduation day, 1925.

Llanfyllin, Sue's birthplace in Wales, photographed in the 1930s.

The view of Saroa from the mission house.

Robert Rankin Jnr aged one year and ten months, with his
friend Sammy.

The old mission house in Saroa, for many years Sue's home, photographed in 1983.

Bob and Sue Rankin outside Saroa Church in 1956, just before they left Saroa.

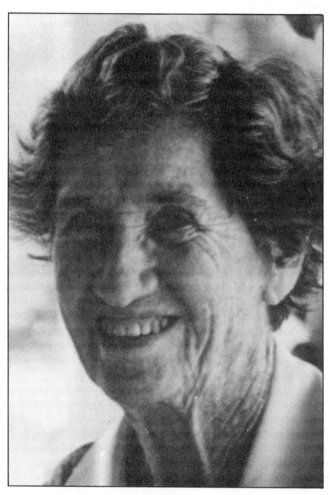

Sue Rankin in 1978.

asked, pointing to the first words. Thinking the Motu was not correct Sue asked, 'How should I have said it?' 'Why didn't you say "my servants"?' said Timo. 'But you aren't my servants, I've been sent to be your servant, Timo,' protested Sue. 'We don't want a servant, we want a mother'. 'All right, you have a mother, but I don't want servants, either, I want men who work together with me', argued Sue.

Then she remembered that Timo took cricket very seriously. 'Like a cricket team, you know'. He smiled and said, 'Yes, I understand, now I'll go and explain it to the others'. Sue's comment:

We criticise the paternalistic system. That's what the people wanted in those days. Though I was much younger than many of the people, whenever I visited one of the Sinaugoro villages the people would shout; 'Boys, girls, come, your grandmother has arrived!'

Timo had been very fond of Mrs Lawes. One day he and Sue were sitting on the floor talking when Sue asked Timo to tell her what Mrs Lawes was like. With a big smile Timo said, 'She was a chatterbox, just like you!' The Motu word he used could mean a gossip, a talker or even a scold, so Sue protested. Timo threw his arm around her shoulder and said, 'But we like it!'

Whenever there was a celebration he was the funny man. He would come to the mission house to borrow a pillow so that he could dress up as a white man. Timo thought all white men should have big corporations, even though Mr Turner and Bob Rankin were quite slim.

On one occasion, Marowaea came to Saroa and invited Sue to a big dance and feast that he was preparing. The missionaries did not usually attend heathen feasts. Bob was in Port Moresby at the time and when Timo came to see her, Sue asked his advice. 'I think you should go to this one', he said.

With Timo, Sue took the half-hour walk down the road to Kwalimurubu and stood near the carved spirit platform in the centre of the village. It was bedecked with sugarcane and bunches of bananas and round the platform were large, bare branches with food tied to them. Each house in the village was festooned with coconut fronds and hibiscus blooms. In front of each house was food ready for the visitors.

Marowaea took his place on the platform. Before he commenced the ceremony he called the people to bring food for their missionary and her boarders. They crowded forward bearing sweet potatoes, yams, bananas and other fruit and vegetables and piled them at Sue's feet. The five Christian families in Kwalimurubu were also given food before it was dedicated to the spirits.

Then the ceremonies started. From the top of the spirit platform the chief named the names of the ancestral spirits of the village over the food. Sue listened intently. She could only hear names. She asked Timo, 'Is he saying anything but names?' 'No, just names'. The visitors from other villages pressed forward as the food and other gifts were shared out according to the chief's instructions.

Marowaea came down from the platform and a little pig was handed to him. He held it in his hands as he named the names of the spirits over it and then let it go. Sue wondered if the naming of the names over the food was a way of giving thanks and the naming of the names over the piglet was a means of asking protection from the spirits.

After the feast Marowaea came to the mission house, sat down with Sue and said, 'I invited you to that feast because I had decided it would be the last feast in my village. I want to join the Seekers' Class and learn how to become a Christian'.

The people of the village were very angry with their chief and tried to poison him. For weeks he only ate food prepared in the mission house by the Rankins' cook, Henry. In spite of the watchfulness of his friends, Marowaea did not live long after he became a Christian.

As Sue pondered the ceremony of 'naming the names' it seemed to her like the first stage of prayer. No petition was made, just the spirits named. Sue thought of the teaching in the Bible about the Name of God. How Moses, when he was sent to free the Israelites, said, 'Whom shall I say sent me?' God gave his name as 'I Am'. She considered how throughout the Bible the Name is given great importance: 'Some trust in chariots and some in horses but we will go in the Name of the Lord'. In the New Testament, too, when John and Peter healed the lame man the council asked them, 'By what authority or by what Name did you cause this miracle?' Peter stated that it was in the Name of Jesus. Sue Ellis Rankin had come to Papua to teach the power of the Name of Jesus, higher than any other name. She was finding that the Papuan people could grasp this truth because they understood the power of other names.

Then Timo became ill. He was in a great deal of pain from arthritis and had to stay in bed. The sorcerers took the opportunity to visit him. They wanted to find out by their magic who was the cause of Timo's illness. The sorcerers claimed that someone must be angry with Timo. He refused to let them practise any magic on him. They came constantly, one by one. At last he said to the South Sea pastor, 'Please give me a Scripture verse to hold onto'. It went up on the wall where he could see it easily with a picture of Jesus that Sue had given him.

Timo recovered. The Rankins persuaded him to retire but whenever he felt well enough, he would help in the school or in any way he could. Particularly when Bob was on patrol and Sue was working on the mission station, Timo would be there to help her.

Sue and the Sinaugoro people had much in common. Although they were hot-tempered, they did not hold grudges. One day Timo said that he wanted to see the missionaries; he seemed to be very angry about something. By the time he got up to the house he was laughing. 'Wasn't I a silly old thing?' he said. The cause of the anger was forgotten.

The people called Sue 'the woman without anger'. In spite of her auburn hair and fiery temper, the storms were quickly over. None of that poisonous anger that caused people to become sick, remained.

Timo loved to preach. He often arrived at the church to take his turn in spite of being in great pain. One morning as well as his white shirt and rami and black tie he had a broad pink cloth wound round his waist. Bob Rankin said, 'You're looking smart this morning, Timo!' and slapped him on the back. The pink cloth was warm. It was there to strap a hot water bottle to Timo's aching back.

When he was too ill to go out, he still kept a close eye on the people going up the hill to the mission house. If someone was going to bring Sue down to a sick child he would say, 'Sinabada has only two legs, you know. Take the child up to her'.

As the faithful pastor became weaker, Sue and Bob visited him daily. Timo brought up the question of death. They asked if he had any fear of death. He pointed to the picture of Christ on the wall and said, 'For many years now I've only been afraid of one thing — afraid of making him ashamed of me'.

After a very bad bout of sickness, it happened that Timo's name was again on the list for Saroa's morning service. Of course no-one expected him to arrive. Sue thought that he wasn't even aware that his name was on the list. When he turned up she said, 'You can't take the service, Timo!' But he said, 'I must, I have something to say'.

What a service that was! His text was Luke 12:49: 'I have come to set fire to the earth, and how I wish it were already kindled!' In Motu the word used for already is 'vaitani' which can also mean altogether or completely. That was how Timo understood it.

Timo said; 'You can see what the fire Jesus brought has done. Many bad old things like fear have gone, but you know that up in our hills it is still very dark. I want you young people to take this Good Story of Jesus Christ up to the people in all those places. Then this good story will burn up all the bad ways, and our district, from the coast to the mountains, will become a garden for God'.

Timo never preached again and not long after that, death came. It was 1941. One of his last words was; 'Don't worry about burying my body. Just throw it in the bush. I won't be in it'. He was buried, not with wailing and a great show of grief, but with singing and joy and praise.

Sue was often delighted by the vividness and expressiveness of the prayers offered by the pastors. Her imagination was fired by retired Pastor Iakobo's prayer one Sunday at Saroa: 'We thank you, Lord, that the vine of your love has been such a long one. It has been long enough to reach from heaven to earth. It has been long enough to reach the white people, but oh, thank you because it has been long enough to reach the black people of Papua, too'.

Pastor Noga was a dramatic little man who just forgot everyone else and talked to his Lord. One Good Friday morning at the Communion Service after the story of the trial and crucifixion had been read, Sue could not resist keeping her eyes open as he prayed:

Marvellous, Lord Jesus, just marvellous. You knew quite well what would happen to you in Jerusalem but you still went there. Could we do that? No fear, no fear (in English). You know we would have run into the hills to hide, but never have gone to Jerusalem. But that is what you did and it amazes us. On that long journey your disciples were squabbling about who was going to be the important one in your Kingdom. You had been teaching them for three years but they were so slow to learn, just like us. But you did not get angry, you were so patient. Then when you came in sight of Jerusalem they put you on a donkey, spread their garments on the ground, cut branches from the trees, waved them and led you up the hill, shouting; 'Hosanna!'

Of course they shouted. Why, there were many who wouldn't have been there at all but for you. There were sick people who were well again because of you, and lame people who could walk because of you, and dumb people who could speak because of you and blind people who could see because of you, and yes, there were dead people alive again because of you. Of course they shouted, why even we Papuan people would have done as much as that. But they forgot again, just like us.

Then you were arrested and all your disciples fled and left you, so you were taken to the court and accused of all sorts of things but you said nothing. Could we do that? You know we'd have protested and shouted, we couldn't keep quiet, but you did, and that, too, amazes us.

All the people shouted for you to be crucified and they scourged you and mocked you and then they put the cross on your shoulder for you to carry up that hill. Lord, we like to think it was a black man who carried your cross that day. We know he didn't want to do it. What did you say to him on the way? He became glad to help you and taught his sons to be your followers.

So on the hilltop they nailed you on that cross and lifted it

74

up for all to see. But even there they mocked you and said: 'If you are God's Son then come down.' But all you said was; 'Father, forgive them for they don't know what they are doing.'

That is something we can't understand. It amazes us. It is beyond our comprehension. We don't know what to say. We have no words. We can only say; 'Lord, thank you.'

Murder!

Chief Aire Kei of Babaga was very different from the gentle Timo. Aire Kei's father was the brave old chief who had set out to prove that 'vada' were people. When he died his son became chief of Babaga village. Aire Kei was a very warlike man and there were no Christians in his village for many years. A few children attended Saroa school and very few people went to the church services and Sunday school held in the village.

Then came a day of near-tragedy. Pastor Simona's ten-year-old son had gone hunting with his father on Saturday and was lost. On Sunday there was no church service in Saroa. All the men were combing the hills and the women preparing food. The search continued till afternoon, when Simona found his son safe in another small village.

While the searchers were resting and having some food Aire Kei and his wife arrived at the steps of the mission house. They wanted to join the Seekers' Class and become Christians. Two more lost people had been found.

Life was very difficult for Aire Kei. Many people in the village were angry with him for joining the church. He told Sue that some of the young men set on him, trying to provoke him to a fight. He admitted that it was a hard job keeping his fists down and remembering that he was a Christian! When his assailants had given him a pounding, they let him go.

The people of Babaga began to respect their chief's decision. Children began attending school regularly at Saroa. Aire's son came to live on the station. Church and Sunday school were well attended and the people were prepared to accept medical treatment from the missionaries. Babaga was becoming a village of Light. Then came the murder.

Bob was away visiting other districts as chairman of P.D.C. Sue was finishing school for the day when Pastor Timo came into the classroom and said, 'Can you come? There's trouble'. Sue asked, 'Who?' Timo replied, 'Aire Kei'.

Sue dismissed her class and went to the office. Timo had closed every shutter so that it was very dark. He pointed to Aire and said, 'He killed a man today'. Sue could not believe it. 'Is he really dead?' 'I think so', answered Timo. Sue told Timo to stay with Aire Kei while she arranged a stretcher party, hopeful of finding the man still alive. As they set off a policeman came up the road from Rigo to arrest Aire Kei. Back they went. The policeman waited in the village while Sue went up the hill and brought the chief down. He held out his hand for the handcuffs and said; 'Put them on, I've done wrong today'.

While her little son clung to Sue's hand, she said a prayer and then Aire and the policeman went off to Rigo. As they went he turned and said, 'Mother, will you come down to the station in the morning?' Sue promised.

Sue was astounded that the people were not as horrified as she was. She had not asked Aire what had happened. The people were full of sympathy for him and told Sue that a man of another tribe had come to work a small manganese mine near Babaga. Being an hospitable man Aire had made friends with him, given him timber for a house, land for a garden and welcomed him into his home. At one time the stranger had to go away and had asked Aire Kei to look after his wife. He did so 'as a sister', the people said.

Later Aire himself went away to Hula and asked the stranger to look after his wife. Things went wrong and when he returned he heard tales that he did not want to believe. The village people said his wife had gone to the garden. He picked up his spear which he always carried ready to kill a pig or wallaby and went to find his wife. In a small bush shelter in the garden he caught them in the act. Flinging his spear he killed the man while his wife ran off into the bush.

Aire came straight to Saroa, told Timo his story, and asked to be taken to 'our mother'. Timo was filled with horror that a Christian could do a thing like that but the village people said, 'But he had to kill him. As soon as that man knew that Aire had found him out he would have killed Aire. Why should the innocent man suffer?'

Next morning Sue walked down to Rigo. The Government Officer was sympathetic to Aire Kei who was a good village chief. When Sue spoke to Aire he asked her to go to Port Moresby with him. He explained that he was not afraid of punishment but that all the policemen were from that man's tribe and he expected them to try to 'pay back' for their compatriate's life. The Government Officer agreed that Aire Kei's life would be at risk and offered to get a canoe with Gabagaba people as crew to make the trip. Sue and her young son and Aire's wife accompanied him to Port Moresby. He was acquitted. The verdict was 'native justice with intense provocation'. Aire Kei was a free man. But that was not to be the end of the story.

Later in the year the church council for the Saroa Boku district met. They were adamant; 'The Bible says, "Thou shalt not kill". Aire Kei has killed. He can no longer be a church member'. Then Pastor Nou Aire of Gabagaba stood up. He reminded the people that not so long ago a youth was not a man till he had killed someone. Then he was allowed to wear the 'siage' head-dress of bird-of-paradise plumes. 'If we drive this man out of the church he will be able to wear the 'siage'. Some of the young men might decide to follow him'. He asked the people if they wanted that old custom revived.

Then he suggested that Aire Kei be put out of the church for a year, that his return would depend on how he treated his wife. If he kept her and was kind to her he would be suspended for only one year. If he sent her away and took another wife he would be out of the church. That would be Aire Kei's decision. Bob asked from the chair, 'Who will tell him of this ruling?' The people replied, 'Our mother will'.

Sue did not go to the village because she knew that everyone would listen to the conversation. She sent a note to Aire Kei saying, 'Please come and see me'. When Aire heard the decision he wept. He did not want to leave the church and had already taken his wife back because he loved her and she was the mother of his son. A year later Aire Kei was back in the church, chosen as a deacon by the church fellowship. His son, Bulina, became a pastor.

Kiragi

Kiragi was the first student Sue accepted from the inland villages while she was still at Kalaigoro. But when he brought his wife to the mission station, she was covered with sipoma. The young missionary explained that they could only be accepted to prepare for entrance to college if Lidia would submit to treatment for the unsightly skin disease. She agreed. First it was necessary to shave her hair. Kiragi and Lidia were with Sue for two years, moving to Saroa with her. The couple had no children. Kiragi was angry about this and often thrashed his wife. He had been disciplined and seemed repentant.

Lidia's skin was clear and it was almost time for the college entrance exams. By this time Sue had married and returned to Saroa with Bob. One afternoon just as guests arrived at the front steps of the mission house Lidia rushed up the back steps covered with blood. Bob was with the guests and Henry had the tea ready to pour. Sue excused herself and cleaned up the poor woman's head. She was very angry. When Bob came to see what was delaying her, Sue said, 'You'll just have to beat him this time'. Bob refused to give the man the punishment Sue thought he deserved. She said, 'Right, I'll do it myself'. Picking up a small cane she used as a pointer in school, she went looking for Kiragi.

She found him on the school playground and said, 'You have been thrashing a woman for a long time; now a woman is going to thrash you. Turn around!' Sue gave him a few good cuts with the cane on his back. Looking up she noticed that Bob and the South Sea pastor were standing by. Kiragi took the beating calmly and Sue, still very angry said, 'I hope you come out in bumps!'

The missionaries walked back up the hill to their visitors and ate dinner with them. By this time Sue was feeling sick with remorse for what she had done and slipped out to go in search of Kiragi. Not finding him in his house or in the village, she retraced her steps slowly up the hill. Bob met her on the doorstep. 'Kiragi is waiting for you in your office'. Sue flopped down in the chair and said to Kiragi, 'Sit down'. But the young man came and knelt down with his head in her lap.

As he wept, Sue wept and said, 'I'm sorry son, I had no right to do that to you'. He replied, 'Sina (mother), don't say "sorry" to me. If you had killed me, that, too, would have been justified'. He and Sue talked about the college course. He promised never to beat his wife again. Then they had a prayer together. When he was leaving he said, 'Sina, will you put something on the bumps?' Feeling very ashamed, Sue asked Bob to treat the bruises. Later Bob made one remark; 'You certainly did a good job on that poor lad!'

It was a rule that no student was to strike his wife, but sometimes the wives said vile things to their husbands. Two students came to Sue one day and asked what they could do when their wives said those things to them. Sue said, 'There is no rule to stop me beating them. If they do it, send them to me'. Sue also found that if a woman in the village had been beaten up, she just had to say to the man, 'You know what I did to Kiragi. If you beat your wife again I will come and do the same to you!' The threat worked!

Kiragi and his very capable wife went to college, completed the course and were appointed to a new village on the Kemp Welch River. Once, at a service there, Sue heard him say, 'Don't say you are too bad to become members of the church of Jesus Christ. I was so bad that Sina had to thrash me'.

The couple were moved to another village and there, too they worked well. After some years there were still no children. Then one day a woman whose marriage had broken up returned to the village. The missionaries heard rumours that Kiragi was becoming friendly with the woman and causing distress to Lidia. They sent for him. He denied that he was doing any more than his pastoral duty, but a few weeks later Bob and Sue received the news that Kiragi had taken the woman as a second wife. That meant that he had to be suspended as a pastor and he went home to Geveragoro with both wives.

Kiragi came again and again begging to be reinstated, but it was against the church rules. He was very unhappy. A child was born and Kiragi wanted to send the mother away and keep that baby with his first wife, and then return to his work as pastor. Again he came, put his head in Sue's lap and wept, but she was not able to do what he wanted and he went away very sad. Within a few months Kiragi had died.

Chapter 9

Fire!

Bob believed that teaching the boys and student pastors carpentry and building skills was as important as teaching the three r's. While Sue supervised the school and taught the students and their wives, preparing them for the college entrance exam, her husband took over the store, the bookkeeping, maintenance of the buildings and teaching carpentry.

There was no church building or school at Gabagaba. The timbers from an old church had been carefully stacked for ten years, ready to use for a new building. Saroa also needed a new church and a school building.

Bob heard that some houses were for sale at an old copper mine at Bootless Bay, between Gabagaba and Port Moresby. After talking to the Saroa and Gabagaba people he made an offer for the buildings which was accepted. He and some Saroa men walked along the coast to demolish the buildings. A hundred pounds had been given to Saroa and Gabagaba by the L.M.S. for their help in moving the college from Vatorata to Fife Bay. This money was used to purchase the buildings at Bootless Bay and other materials necessary to build two churches. When the houses had been pulled down the Gabagaba men took their big canoes along to bring the timber back.

Plans for two churches were drawn up in a cruciform style. Nou Airi was in charge of the work at Gabagaba and Bob supervised the building at Saroa. The posts had been cut and brought to the site at Saroa and the time had come to commence building. The day before the post holes were to be dug and the posts fixed in the ground all the women went to the garden to bring back plenty of vegetables and the men went hunting.

Eve, Bob and Sue and two South Sea pastors were going about their normal work on the mission station with the school children. The village was deserted except for one young woman who was ill, and her little girl. During the afternoon the little girl demanded something which her mother refused and the child picked up a firestick, kept glowing to light the fire, and put it to the thatch of the house.

The frantic mother snatched up her child and ran to Babaga village shouting, 'Fire!' The missionaries saw the smoke and ran to the village but they were helpless. There was a strong wind and the fire spread rapidly. The men tried to save some of the precious floor boards of the houses but they were nailed down rather than tied with vines as in the past and could not be moved. The lower half of the village was burnt to the ground.

The missionaries hurried back to the station to prepare accommodation in the schoolroom and prepare a meal for the homeless people. When the women returned and found their homes gone, they wept. Men and women stood around shocked, unable to move. Then Sue saw a very tall man turn and ask a question. He picked up his spear and set off for Babaga. She knew immediately what was in his mind, sprinted after him and clung to his arm. 'No Mairi, don't do it, it won't help'. Ignoring her he strode to the end of the village, with the slight woman still dragging at his arm. Suddenly he stopped, turned and smiled and said, 'You're right, we'll go back'. Sue let out a sob of relief. There would be no pay-back. The child and her mother were safe.

It was a very sad night as Sue and Bob cared for the homeless and listened to their bewildered conversations. The missionaries assumed that the work planned for the next morning would be postponed while the houses were rebuilt. But: 'Was it God's fault?' the people asked indignantly. 'No! Then why should he suffer?'

Early next morning the work of digging holes and fixing posts for the church started. But there were some murmurings of disappointment among the Saroa people that the Gidobada people had not come to help as they had promised. However, during the morning the men and women of Gidobada arrived, laden with vegetables. Having heard of the fire they had all gone out to their gardens at day-break to get extra supplies of food for their neighbours in Saroa.

While the church was going up some of the men built small huts to house their families till they could start preparing materials to build new houses. Once a year the Administration gave a five-pound prize to the best-kept village. There was a lot of competition among the villages as this prize was the only cash that came into a village at that time. The District Officer decided to give the prize to the Saroa people to encourage them. The money was presented to the village councillors and during the week it was shared out among all the families. To the amazement of the missionaries the people decided to give the money towards the new church. At the service on Sunday morning the people brought their gifts and every penny of that five pounds was given to the church fund.

The first few posts brought in for the church were carved with old Papuan designs. Sue admired the old designs but the church members were adamant that none of the old heathen carving could be used on God's house.

Bob and Sue went on one of their inland patrols. Nou Airi had reached the stage of fixing the timbers for the cruciform roof of the Gabagaba church. He could not understand how to do it. Though he was far from young and had only one good eye, he walked up to Saroa. Accepting only a drink from the Samoan pastor he climbed the ladder to see how Bob had done the roof of the Saroa church, took measurements, climbed down and walked back to Gabagaba to complete his work.

In the old church building at Saroa the services had been very noisy affairs. Everybody laughed and talked coming in to church. It was hard to get the service started. Sue took her gramophone down to the church and had one of the deacons play records till the service started. The people enjoyed the music and with one deacon on the church steps to remind them to be quiet, they came in and sat quietly before the service.

The new Saroa church was to be named the Angas Memorial Church as a reminder that the inland work of the Saroa district had been started with a gift from Mr Angas of South Australia.

One Sunday afternoon Sue and Bob went to Gabagaba where a meeting was to be held to choose a name for the Gabagaba church. When many names had been suggested, Nou Airi stood up and said that one name for Jesus in the Book of Revelation was, 'The Morning Star'. 'I would like that name for the church', he said. Suddenly in the sleepy heat of the afternoon the whole meeting came alive. 'Yes, of course', said the people, 'that is the right name'.

Bob and Sue did not understand how the matter had been settled so suddenly. Later, in the pastor's house, they asked Nou Airi why he had chosen that name. He showed them two verses in Revelation, 2:28 and 22:16. Then he explained that in the old days when they had no clocks they told the time by the sun and the stars. They were seafarers and to them the most important star was the morning star. The evening before starting on a voyage the canoe could be prepared, all the cargo stowed away, food, water, firewood loaded and all the crew would sleep on board. As soon as the morning star rose, the watch would wake the crew and the canoe set sail in the thick darkness. The sailors knew that the sun would rise within a short time. The morning star was always the herald of the dawn. Nou said that that name would remind his people that Jesus Christ the Morning Star had come. Although there was much darkness along the coast of Papua, a few fingers of light were showing. If the people were faithful to Jesus Christ one day the whole land would be full of light.

The people also used a seafaring term in Motu to describe repentance. When they became Christians they said, 'I will now right about face and walk in the opposite direction in my thinking'. Sue asked an old pastor where the term came from. He said he thought it was an expression from the days when the Motu people went trading for sago in the west on the hiri expeditions. The men sailed west with the south-east wind and stayed some months in the Gulf exchanging their pots for sago and other food. When the wind changed they started to think about sailing home. With the nor'west wind behind them, they sailed back in the opposite direction. 'Helalo kerehai' means 'think about face'. The people said that they had been walking away from God and now the light had come they would turn around and walk with God.

In September 1937 the Rev. R. L. and Mrs Turner came to visit the district and opened the two churches. It was a wonderful reunion with the missionaries who had taken Dr Lawes' place and worked in the district till 1924.

Sue began putting even more effort into teaching the people to read in their own vernacular.

While Sue was polishing up her Motu again and helping Bob to make the change from using the Toaripi language of the Gulf to Motu, she was glad to have services and school vernacular classes in that language. But she believed that people should worship in their own language, and that the children should learn to read their own language first.

She asked the Saroa people, 'Do you say your prayers at home in Motu?' 'No', they answered, 'we use Sinaugoro'. 'Why can't we have our services in Sinaugoro?' she suggested. Sue began to teach the youngest children in the school to read Sinaugoro. Gradually Sinaugoro prayers were introduced into the services. At one of the church council meetings the people said they wanted their children to learn to read Motu and English, not Sinaugoro, but Sue persisted. She learnt Sinaugoro from the little children in the school and started to write a simple reading book for them.

Sue had already written a Motu primer for the small children which also contained stories and legends. With the help of Pastor

Timo's son Henry, who was her cook, she prepared blackboard work in Sinaugoro and gradually built up a Sinaugoro primer. Henry helped her write down some of the Saroa legends which were mainly stories telling 'why'. A visitor remarked to Bob that all the children spoke Motu with a rising inflection: 'Of course,' said Bob, 'they were taught by my wife!'

As each new area was opened up Sue started to jot down the words she could hear from the new languages. As the pastors learnt the new vernacular they helped her till she had written primers in the Kware, Mount Brown, Barai and Doromu languages. She was convinced that the people should learn to read in their own language first.

Sue felt that the people needed something to read besides their New Testament in Motu. She decided to translate a simple version of *Pilgrim's Progress*. As it was translated chapter by chapter it appeared in a small newspaper called *Harina* or *News* that was distributed from Port Moresby.

It was difficult to work on writing at Saroa because people were coming and going all day long. When Sue needed time for translation or preparing a booklet for publication she would retreat to the Nicholson's house at Kokebagu for a week. Her hosts provided a room for her use and only called her at meal times. At half-past four Mrs Nicholson would say, 'It's time for a walk'. Sue would stop work, have a cup of tea and go for a walk with her. *Pilgrim's Progress* was published in 1948 with illustrations by the Rev. Bert Brown.

In 1934 the educational work was very important. Missions conducted the only schools in Papua. Wherever a pastor was placed, a small village school was commenced. The children were taught simple arithmetic, reading and writing in Motu and then went on to learn a little English. At the annual collection meetings each June, Sue and Bob held an examination in Motu including recitation of some Scriptures and some questions on the parables. Prizes were given to the best scholars and an L.M.S. flag and extra school materials to the best schools.

By 1939 the missionaries were examining the children in their villages and inspecting the schools during their patrols.

The school at Saroa was for children from Saroa and Gidobada as well as the boarders who lived on the mission station. Some of the boarders were pastors' children, some were from heathen villages and had little knowledge of living on a mission station or Christian teaching. Some girls lived in the Rankins' house, others with the South Sea pastor and his wife. The boys had a large house and their own kitchen. The student-pastors lived in a three-roomed house with an outside kitchen.

All the station people bathed in the creek at the bottom of the hill and depended on two large tanks at the mission station for water for cooking. The missionaries' bath water went into a large drum and was used for watering plants.

The children from Babaga and Kemaea attended school at Kwalimurubu. One pastor and his wife conducted each school. Sue suggested that the five villages combine in a school at Saroa. The children and their teachers walked to Saroa each day carrying their lunch wrapped up in banana leaves. The bundles of sweet potato, cooked bananas, sago balls or other cooked vegetables were hung in a tree away from the always-hungry village dogs. Each village had its own tree and at lunch time one child would climb and hand down the packages. After school each day the children had games.

The parents were very happy with the new arrangement and soon Sue suggested that school be held four days a week because the work learned on Mondays and Tuesdays was often forgotten by Thursdays! Again the parents consented.

Friday was supposed to be the day when the children learned about their own culture from their parents. The girls went to the garden with their mothers, but the boys, who should have been hunting with their fathers, usually played around the village. The missionaries used Fridays for sending the boarders to the garden, for painting, repair work and new building.

Sue started a youth group with 'L.M.S.' as its name meaning 'Let Me Serve'. Their promise was; 'Whom will you serve?'

I will serve My Lord
My Master
and My Saviour.

Later an L.M.S. youth group was formed for the whole of Papua and named Torchbearers.

The pupils from Gabagaba and Saroa schools sat for exams set by the Government while Sue set the exams for the inland children. On the strength of the Government exams some funds were given to the mission, half a crown (twenty-five cents) a year for each child who had passed standard one, five shillings (fifty cents) for standard two, seven and six (seventy-five cents) for standard three, ten shillings (one dollar) for standard four, and fifteen shillings (one dollar fifty) for standard five. Then the Government said that no one mission could earn more than two hundred and fifty pounds (five hundred dollars) a year. Port Moresby and Hula both had big schools so Saroa district received about twenty-five pounds (fifty dollars) a year.

Mission gifts sent by churches in Britain and Australia provided school materials which Sue was able to share out among the teachers. When the Saroa people started to earn cash they refused the books and pencils saying, 'We can afford to pay for books and pencils now, give these to the inland people'. So each Saroa child bought his own pencil, rubber, ruler and exercise book.

One Sunday morning after church at Saroa the Europeans of the district had been invited to meet the Rev. Norman Goodall and the Rev. Leonard Hurst of the L.M.S. board. Ivan Champion and the school inspector were also present. While Mr Champion was explaining to the board members the large amount of help the Government was giving the mission in education, the school inspector was heard to mutter; 'Yes, less than a farthing a head!' A farthing was worth about a quarter of a cent.

Patrolling

As the Rankins' son grew, his playmates were the schoolboys living on the station. He spoke their languages more often than he spoke English. When the boys went off to school, he would go down to visit the Samoan pastor and his wife or Pastor Timo who had retired and returned to Saroa. There were plenty of small children in the village and young Bob was never lonely. If he wanted a coconut someone would go up a tree for him.

When Sue protested because Bob always spoke in Motu or Sinaugoro to his parents, he replied in Motu, 'What is the L.M.S. language, then?'

The missionaries found travelling with the carriers on their patrols lots of fun. They would walk for two hours and then rest near a creek or river for half an hour. At the first stop of the day rice would be cooked for the carriers in kerosene drums and a kettle boiled for tea. There was always someone to make a bit of fun. On most of the trips it was the chief from Dirikomana who would suddenly disappear and come back dressed up in some way and act the fool. He was very funny and no matter how tired they were the whole party would soon be roaring with laughter.

The Papuans loved to make jokes about the white people and to imitate them. While Sue and Bob were on leave on one occasion, Percy Chatterton relieved them at Saroa. He heard tales from the people about Mr Short who was about six feet two and very heavy. The people were joking because he was always wanting to stop to boil the billy. When Sue heard Percy telling these jokes at Committee she could not resist adding to the tales. She told how after Percy had been at Saroa, she was on patrol when at a certain place near a river, Vetari flung himself on the ground and started gasping, 'Water! Water!' Sue thought he was suffering from sunstroke.

There was a great burst of laughter and he said, 'That's what Mr Chatterton did when he got here!'

One of the carriers always travelled round wearing a pair of men's long johns. Early in the cold mornings he would have them rolled down his legs. As the day went on they would be rolled higher and higher till they were right up. When evening fell the missionaries were always amused to see them gradually rolled down again.

The village people were always hospitable and had food prepared for their missionaries and carriers. In the inland villages where pots were not common the food was cooked by roasting in the embers or in a stone oven. As they acquired cooking pots they would add a few greens such as pumpkin tops to the diet.

Medical supplies were always an important part of the patrol equipment. There was no-one else to do medical work and the need was very great. In the Wiga group of villages were many people with enlarged thyroid glands. Sue and Bob arranged to get some medicine from the chief medical officer and spent a week in the village treating the people twice a day. Then they taught the pastor to continue the treatment. A great improvement was seen in the people's health.

As they continued their patrol, Sue and Bob would stop for a short while at each village, have a rest and a chat to the people and treat a few sick people. There were centres where they usually slept and the people from the other villages would gather there for a day of celebrations.

The pattern of Sue's earlier patrols continued. After a cup of tea and a short rest, Sue played games with the women and children while Bob talked to the older men or played cricket with the younger men. Then the people went to get their meal and came back again to spend the evening. After singing and stories and evening prayers the women took the children home to bed and the men stayed to talk. This was the time for deeper teaching of the Gospel and answering the many questions that were in the people's minds.

As they walked the trails Bob and Sue learnt many stories and skills from their carriers. On coming to a meeting of several tracks they wondered which one to take. The carriers gathered round a pile of sticks, stones and leaves on the path. After talking among themselves they said, 'Now we know the way'. They explained that the heap of sticks, stones and leaves was like a letter. The stones had been arranged so as to close off the other tracks. One stick had been placed to show the right way and a leaf placed on top of the heap said it was a message from their tribe, a sort of signature. The information was correct.

For a while after her return to Papua with her son, Bob insisted on Sue being carried when they went on patrol. Four men carried a chair tied to two poles. Bob junior was carried in a small chair by two men. When he was sleepy he rode on Sue's lap. Sue hated being carried. The men did it with great enthusiasm. Running through the creeks and rivers they shouted, 'This is the inland lorry. It doesn't use benzine (petrol) and it doesn't have punctures!'

The men made a chair of heavy timber with railing sides. Sue's bedroll went into it and they wanted her to sit on top of it. It was like being in a cage. As the men trotted along the jungle tracks Sue rolled from side to side. Fortunately it soon fell apart. On every patrol a chair was carried for Sue but she preferred to walk. Sometimes the men ran over the rough places and stood in front of Sue with the chair insisting that she sit in it. She finally came to an agreement with them that she would walk the steepest, most dangerous places with someone holding her arm, or a hand in the small of her back, and allow them to carry her on the less precipitous parts.

Chapter 10

War

In the year 1937, after ten years of service for Bob, it was time for the family to take a year's leave in Great Britain. They went first to Llanfyllin where Bob junior went to school for a while and made some Welsh friends. The people of the town made a great fuss of him and on market days he was given many pennies. Sue gave him a mission box and suggested that half his pennies be put away for the L.M.S. The second half of their leave was spent in Glasgow. Bob junior was introduced to a new set of relatives.

Before returning to Papua, Bob and Sue went back to Llanfyllin to say goodbye to Sue's family. While he was being put to bed one night the little boy said to his mother, 'I'm afraid of that black man'. Sue was about to say there was no black man in Llanfyllin when she remembered that an Indian man was selling manchester goods from village to village. She said, 'That man isn't black, he is brown like the people of Saroa'. Up sat Bob. 'The people of Saroa are not brown'. 'Yes they are, Uncle Simona is brown', Sue remonstrated. 'No Mammy, he is NOT!' 'Well, Uncle Timo is brown'. 'No Mammy he is NOT!' 'Your friend Baroa is brown.' 'No, he is not. All right Mammy, when we get back you will see!' wagging his finger at his mother.

They returned to Sydney on a small ship carrying twelve passengers. Then to Port Moresby by *John Williams* and to Gabagaba by canoe. When they stopped at the trade store at Rigo on their way to Saroa many people crowded round to greet their missionaries. Bob moved close to his mother and whispered, 'They ARE brown'.

While the family were on leave, Pastor Simona had become ill and it was thought best to send him home. He and Faauma had been in Papua since 1910. Simona left a note for Sue saying that they would not meet again on earth 'but there is a meeting-again place. We will see you there'.

After the Rankins' return Pastor Nou Airi of Gabagaba died. It was decided to move Sepania and Soara from Dirinomu to Gabagaba. At first the people refused to have them but eventually the couple were able to settle in Gabagaba. Months later the village leaders came to thank their missionaries, 'It is evident that you knew what was best for us,' they said. Sepania was a born leader, energetic, vigorous, very thoughtful to the people and as good a sailor as any of the Gabagaba men.

Two little mixed-race boys, brothers, John and George, joined the family, sharing Bob's room and all his toys. John was quick to learn and often asked Bob, who was also five, questions. 'This God, where he live?' Sue heard him say. 'He lives everywhere, John. He is looking at you now and if you go to some other place he'll be there, too', replied Bob. Another day it was; 'Jesus, he what?' Bob answered, 'Oh, John, he was the nicest man who ever lived. If you had bad eyes, John, he would touch them and they'd be better at once'.

Then came news of the war and the little boys were talking. Said John; 'Soldiers marching!' Bob replied. 'Yes, it's those Germany people'. That night he had a new prayer; 'Those Germany people, God, wanting to fight. You just give it to them!'

Sue remonstrated with him. 'I don't think God would like that prayer'. 'Why?' asked Bob. 'He's not like that,' answered Sue, 'he doesn't "give it" to people and besides, he loves those Germany people as much as he loves us'.

There was a long pause then down went the little head; 'Don't listen to that prayer, God, just love the Germany people, that's all'. As the news of the war got worse the prayer to God to bless even those Germany people went on, but there was an addition; 'But don't let them win!'

Bob had been enrolled in correspondence school from Tasmania but Sue found it difficult to supervise him and continue the two senior classes that she was teaching. Bob was far more interested in what his friends were doing than in working by himself at his lessons.

It was time for the agonising decision that missionary parents face. Should they send Bob to boarding school? Some parents chose to send their children back to Great Britain, which meant they were near relatives but would only see their parents every six years. Bob and Sue decided on Melbourne.

It was 1940. War was imminent in the Pacific. Bob was seven and a half and his parents were due for four months leave in Melbourne. But missionaries were asked not to take their leave unless they needed medical treatment. It was decided that the small boy should travel to Melbourne with two missionary families. He was very upset at leaving his parents till they assured him that his Aunt Eve would be there to meet him. Bob considered Eve his second mother.

Five of Bob's friends went with the family to Port Moresby to farewell him. Then came the most painful day of Sue's life. She and Bob took their son and his friends down to the ship. They were not allowed onto the wharf because of wartime restrictions. At the gate they gave him into the care of their friends and turned and went back to Metoreia. The five little boys refused to move but sat weeping outside the gate till the sun went down. From the veranda of the mission house, Bob and Sue watched the ship carrying their son leave Port Moresby Harbour.

Just before Bob had left, his two little mixed-race friends were taken away from the Rankins. Their father was a Roman Catholic and their mother belonged to the L.M.S. There had been a family squabble and the little boys were taken to Port Moresby and sent to Yule Island Catholic Mission. Later they were put on a boat taking mixed-race people to the west for safety. The ship was torpedoed and all were lost.

The house at Saroa was very empty. All Bob's young friends were grieving and everything reminded Sue and Bob of their son. They packed up and set out on an inland patrol, taking young Bob's collie dog with them. For days the dog searched for his young master, running backwards and forwards from Sue to Bob. After traversing the rough limestone country on the banks of the Kemp Welch, they came to the Hunter River. The dog refused to swim across but stood howling on the river's edge. Two of the carriers retraced their steps and carried him across. They found that his paws were badly cut by the spikes of limestone. Sue bandaged them, but he was still in great pain. Glad of an excuse to walk, Sue suggested that the carriers put the dog in her chair.

During the trip the Ikeaga people told Sue and Bob of their concern for the Mount Brown people. Men from the Mount Brown villages often stayed in the Ikeaga villages on their way to and from the coast and the Ikeaga people talked to them of Christ and the Christian way of life. The Mount Brown people knew the quality of the Ikeaga people's lives. One village sent representatives to Saroa to ask for a pastor. Sue, aware of the usual motives for wanting a pastor to work in a village, asked, 'Why do you want a pastor? Is

91

it because the other villages have one, or to get medical care, or to have your children taught to read and write?' They replied, 'We can see the Ikeaga people; they live good lives, they don't steal, they don't commit adultery, they don't practice magic. We want someone to teach us to be like them'.

Comforted in their grief for their son by their Papuan friends, the Rankins returned to Saroa and the work of the mission station. Their plans for visiting Mount Brown were thwarted by the invasion of Papua by the Japanese. It was 1947 before their dream was fulfilled.

All women and children are to be evacuated

Life was very uncertain for expatriates in Papua at the end of 1941. People were saying that the Japanese would never cross the Owen Stanley Range, but Sue and Bob knew this was a false hope. They had no illusions about the ability of the Owen Stanleys to stop the invaders.

Then came the call for all women and children to be evacuated. Sue and Bob discussed the possibility of Sue taking the South Sea women and children inland. There were no arrangements for their evacuation and the missionaries were concerned for their safety. It was decided that Sue should pack tinned food and other provisions and prepare to go to a school house on the Kemp Welch River with her protegees. She knew the area better than any other foreigner and was sure that they would be safe there. It was decided to move after Christmas.

Christmas was just over when the other white men of the district came to Bob. They were concerned about Mr Heiner, the manager of the government rubber plantation. His wife had already gone to Australia and Mr Heiner was very ill with asthma and a duodenal ulcer. Bob was asked to take him to Port Moresby and arrange for him to join his wife.

During her husband's short absence, Sue listened carefully for radio messages. The news from Milne Bay and the north coast was not good. The Japanese were having some success. She called the South Sea pastors' wives together and told them to pack, ready to leave for the Kemp Welch River. They were almost ready to leave when Bob arrived.

'Did you hear the radio message for you?' he asked Sue. She had been ordered to go to Port Moresby, prepared to fly to Cairns. Sue pleaded with Bob that she should fulfil her responsibility to the pastors' wives. She had almost persuaded him to let her go when a truck arrived bringing Mrs Short, who had arrived by canoe at Gabagaba from Hula. Mr Short had heard the radio message and had sent his wife to accompany Sue to Port Moresby.

Still hoping that she might be allowed to return to Saroa, Sue consented to go with Mrs Short. Word quickly went round the villages that Sinabada was leaving. Councillors and deacons arrived to reassure her. 'You go and don't worry, we'll look after the work'.

Arriving in Port Moresby they found that Gwen Ure from Metoreia had already flown to Cairns, and Mrs Nixon from Fife Bay and Mrs Gilkison and baby from Mailu had just arrived. Sue went to see Len Murray, the Administrator, hoping for permission to stay, but he convinced her that she should go. The women were told to hold themselves ready to fly to Cairns at short notice. Two days later the order came; 'Be at the airport in half an hour'.

How does one say goodbye not knowing what the future will bring? Bob stood on the airstrip watching the plane recede into the distance. All those things he had left unsaid to his beloved wife. She might fit under his raised arm but she was like a powerhouse to him. He turned away imagining the long, slow train trip from Cairns to Melbourne. How would they manage? Who would feed them? Would they have enough money? Sue comments;

What a welcome the Cairns folk gave us! They housed us at the Railway Hotel and provided food at a nearby restaurant. We were not allowed to pay a penny. They refused our offers with, 'We may be next'. We shall always be grateful to the people of Cairns.

After a few days in Cairns the travellers boarded the train for Brisbane and Sydney. When they arrived in Sydney, Sue was lifting luggage down from the rack when Ngaire Gilkison, overwhelmed, cried, 'Oh, Sue!' and flung her arms round her. When she arrived in New Zealand, Ngaire found that about the time they had arrived in Sydney her husband had died of blackwater fever at Mailu.

The Port Moresby mission station was taken over by the Army. Eric Ure moved to Saroa with Bob Rankin. They were allowed to patrol the villages east to Hula where Mr Short was holding the fort, and west to Delena where Percy Chatterton was in charge. The people of the villages near Port Moresby had been evacuated east and west and Bob and Eric kept in touch with them. The Army asked the two men to become chaplains but they refused, preferring to stay with their own people. Late in 1942 a party of traders and planters walked over the Owen Stanley Range from New Guinea. They had escaped from the Japanese and pleaded with Bob and Eric to go to Australia with them.

Longing to see their wives and families, the two men considered the offer and then decided to stay. As they again farewelled a plane from Jackson's airstrip, the loneliness was almost more than they could bear. The normal work of the mission was much heavier without wives to share it. The never-ending medical treatments, the school routine, difficulties in getting supplies, made each day more exhausting. When the Army arranged for Percy, Bob and Eric to have a few months' leave with their families in Australia they accepted with relief.

Meanwhile Gwen Ure and Sue had continued their journey from Sydney to Melbourne together. Sue thought of her husband at Saroa encouraging and comforting the people and her nine-year-old son Bob waiting for her in Melbourne. His first words when they stepped off the train were; 'Mammy you are so small!' Mother and son were to be together for two years. It had been planned for the boy to spend Christmas at Saroa that year but it was another three years before he was able to return to Papua.

In Melbourne she settled down in Camberwell and Bob returned to boarding school, coming home to Sue for weekends. They both welcomed Father enthusiastically when he arrived for a break in 1943.

People everywhere were interested in Sue's stories of Papua. Many wounded Australian soldiers had written home of the help and love given to them by the 'fuzzy wuzzy angels'. Sue was often asked, 'What can we do for these people after the war?' One Australian woman who had been a resident of New Guinea wrote to the Australian papers saying that a great feast should be made. Each carrier should be given a small bag of presents — soap, tobacco etc. Sinabada Rankin was incensed!

That evening she was attending a meeting in Collins Street Independent Church, Melbourne. The chairwoman, who had been an L.M.S. missionary, invited Sue to speak: 'I see Mrs Rankin is here. Perhaps she would like to comment on the letter in the paper this morning'.

Sue rose to her feet. 'What do you think these Papuans are? They are people just like us. They need the same things, not feasts and dilly bags, but help with education and medicine'.

After the meeting a few people met with Sue and discussed what could be done to help the Papuan people. They brought out four points:

1. A pro-Papuan government. Sue says;

Being a Welsh nationalist the government came first for me. I felt that the Papuans should be part of the Government and have their wishes taken into account. Before the war even in the church the whites made all the decisions. I could see them being treated as we Welsh were, and that in their own country.

94

Later I was accused of saying that we should all leave and give the country back to the Papuans. I simply said that in Papua, Papuans should be put first.

2. Help with education. The missions were bearing the brunt of the educational work with very small grants from the government.
3. Help with health. Once again the missions were doing the larger part of the medical work.
4. Careful scrutiny of the credentials of those coming into the country. Sue;

To get into Papua in those days was easy. It was often a haven for drop-outs and lazy men. They came in, went to a village and the people were always kind to them. Often they found good Papuan women and settled down with them, leaving the provisioning to their Papuan wives. I thought only people who would make a contribution to the country should be allowed in, not drones and drunkards.

Late in 1943 Sue was sent to Canberra to speak on the work in Papua. News of her statements had filtered to the top. She arrived to be told that she was expected at the Governor-General's residence for tea. A neighbour lent Sue her new fur coat, so she arrived at the residence looking a very prosperous missionary! Lord Gowrie came straight to the point; 'You have been saying some interesting things. I'd like you to tell me what they are'.

Sue told him of her anger at the feast-and-dilly-bag idea and of the urgent need for help in education and health. She pleaded for a government that had the interests of the people at heart as it had been in the days of Sir Hubert Murray, and suggested careful screening of people who wanted to reside in Papua. She then asked permission to make one more point. It was granted. 'Although they are good honest officers, many of the government men have not reached matriculation. I believe the educational standard should be raised'.

Lord Gowrie was very interested in all Sue had to say and the 'ordeal' turned out to be a very pleasant afternoon. Sue's vivid descriptions and evident love and respect for the Papuan people opened the eyes of the people in Canberra. She visited the second in command in the Foreign Affairs Department on behalf of her people. She felt they were being exploited by the Army. In the trade stores (which had been taken over by the Army) the price of tobacco had increased 100 per cent and no food, saucepans or towels were available. When Sue returned to Papua she found the Army were running a trade store at which as well as tobacco, food, towels, and saucepans were sold at a reasonable price. She took every opportunity to promote the interests of the Papuan people.

The opening of the School of Pacific Administration at Mosman, Sydney, after the war encouraged her greatly.

Sue was impatient to get back to her people. It was good to have her son's company and to share her enthusiasm for Papua with the people of Australia, but she could picture the impossible burden that the men were bearing. She had to get back. She even wrote to ex-Prime Minister Billy Hughes, asking him to plead her cause. Surely a Welshman would understand.

Chapter 11

Back to Saroa

Eventually Sue, Chrissie Chatterton and a Seventh Day Adventist missionary were allowed to return to resume their educational work. While waiting at Metoreia for transport to their stations, Sue met Miss Camilla Wedgwood who, with the rank of colonel, had been sent by the Army to inspect and report on the schools in Papua. On observing the people of the villages taking part in church services, using hymn books and reading Bible passages, she came to the conclusion that eighty-three per cent of the people were literate. This gratified Sue because most of the schools belonged to the L.M.S.

Many buildings in Port Moresby had been looted during the owners' absence and an Army officer asked Sue if she could identify an organ they had found. It was from Ela Church.

Eventually Percy Chatterton arrived in Port Moresby to claim his wife and Bob Rankin and Eric Ure arrived to take Sue home. Sue says, 'I received a wonderful welcome; people from villages I had never visited arrived to greet me. They were convinced that because I had come home the war was over'.

One by one the Rankin's expatriate friends returned and settled down to work. The Nicholsons and Heiners were back but some plantations had new managers and the government officers were transferred regularly.

Mr Nicholson told Sue, 'I wish I had listened to you when you talked about the people being afraid of that spirit mountain, Durigolo'. He said that while Bob was in Melbourne he had taken carriers over the range to the north coast with supplies, and brought back wounded. 'When we were near Durigolo, only the Christians would go on. All the others dropped their packages and fled. If only I had talked to them beforehand perhaps they would have gone on'. Sue knew that the people were afraid because they said the spirits were always unhappy on the cold, wet mountain and were looking for a way to escape. In the old days the people believed that the spirits of the dead stayed near their home for about three days and then went to the spirit mountain, Durigolo, which could be seen from Boku. During the days when the spirits were still supposed to be around the house, the people were very frightened.

Back to teaching Sue went. Getting the schools going again took a great deal of time. There were three hundred children in Saroa school, made up of the children from five local villages and boarders from inland who lived on the mission station.

The eyes of the missionaries were again turning towards the inland areas of the Barai and Mount Brown. Deputations were becoming frequent — 'We have come to ask for a teacher for our village. We want to learn the Way of Jesus and have our children taught to read and write'. The deputation of betel-nut-stained men sat cross-legged on the veranda of the mission house.

Sue or Bob sat on the floor with their visitors and talked to them about their village. Where was it? What language group did they belong to? How many people were in the village? Why did they want a pastor? Then the missionary said, 'If you want a teacher for your village go home and build a house for him and make a garden, then come back to us'. It was explained that the village would be expected to give some money each year towards their teacher's support.

Usually the deputation returned a few months later. 'We have built a house and planted a food garden. We have come to take our teacher home now'. Sometimes there was a man from one of the Sinaugoro villages who was willing to take his family to an inland village and teach the people about Jesus. As some of the students graduated from Lawes' College they were placed in the villages but often there was just no-one to send.

Just as Gabagaba village was settling down after the disruption of the war the people decided to have a large feast. The missionaries were concerned. This would mean no school for the children for a month in which the entire village would dance all night and sleep all day. A retired medical orderly also told Sue and Bob that the dance would be a 'splendid help' in the spread of venereal disease.

Pastor Sepania had left, the senior deacon had died and a new Samoan Pastor, Alesana, had just arrived. Would the Christians be able to stand the test? The village people pressed them to accept the food which had been offered to the spirits and to join in the dance, but with Alesana's encouragement, the Christians stood firm.

Sue always regretted that some of the dances could not be used as folk dances. When a Kwalimurubu man who had been a dance leader became a Christian she asked him, 'Isn't there one dance that we could use on special days of celebration?' He replied, 'I know all the dances in all the villages and there is not one dance clean enough to be brought into the church'.

At the opening of a new church building at Saroa the church leaders allowed the dancing of an old legend. It depicted the story of Guru Fore and Gamada Fore, coming up through the rocks at Taboro Goro to see the beautiful world and going back to bring all their people to live in the light. That dance was only performed once by the Christians. To replace the dancing connected with spirit worship, the South Sea pastors and their wives taught the children their graceful dances and the boys also learnt the vigorous dances of the Kiwai men of the Western District.

Mr Nicholson of Kokebagu decided to use his labour and equipment to plant rice. Bob took the students up to help with the planting and offered to help with the reaping. It was a good crop.

Later, Mr Nicholson talked to Bob Rankin about growing rice on a commercial basis. They went to see the Saroakei people just across the river from the plantation. Mr Nicholson suggested that they lend him some of their kunai-covered river bank in return for cheap rice. The people agreed and the missionaries and plantation manager felt that this could be the beginning of an industry for the Saroakei people.

The proposal was submitted to the government. Permission was refused. It was not possible for Mr Nicholson to lease the land; the people must sell it to the government for sixpence (five cents) an acre. Then perhaps Mr Nicholson could buy it or lease it from the government. Neither the Rankins nor Mr Nicholson would agree to persuading the people to sell their land, and the project was dropped.

Chapter 12

Women come into their own

Papua was a man's world. The women did most of the garden work, carrying the vegetables home and carrying the water for their cooking. Not that the men were lazy. They were the hunters, the fishermen, they cleared the gardens and made the fences after the burn off. Every five years or so they had to rebuild or at least rethatch their houses. They also made spears, nets and tools.

When a girl married, her husband shaved her head to take away her good looks. But if a girl decided to become a Christian and join the Seekers' Class, her hair was not shaved because becoming a Christian was taken as a sign that she would be faithful to her husband.

Women did not take part in church services. Sue asked if the women could have a service once a month on a Sunday afternoon. The men agreed and offered to have their service in the village street while the women met in the school building, which at that time served as a church also. At first the women would say the prayers or lead the service and Sue or the pastor's wife would give a talk. But gradually the women gained confidence.

One afternoon the widow of an old pastor was speaking. She was called 'Vabu Isaako' (widow of Isaac). She began by reading the story of the Resurrection in Mark's Gospel. When she had finished reading she said:

If Jesus Christ had died and we had heard that story we'd have said; 'Poor man! How kind he was, how cruel those people were to him!' and then we'd have gone away and forgotten all about it. But the story didn't finish there. Jesus rose from the dead and so we know that he is still alive and can still do the things he did on earth.

He can help us just as he did people then. So, whenever I am in trouble — if someone has been angry with me or unkind to me or I need something badly — I go to my room, read that story and say to myself, 'Jesus can help me'. I just tell him all about it and then I feel better and get up and go on with my work.

All I want to say to you is; you do the same. If you are unhappy, if your husband has been unkind to you, if your children have been naughty or someone has said something to hurt you, just read that story and remember that Jesus is still alive and can help you. Just sit down and tell him all about it and then you'll feel happy again.

A knotty problem was being discussed at the all-male deacon's meeting at Saroa. 'Why don't you ask your wives what they think?' suggested Bob Rankin. 'They aren't leaders in the church,' objected one man. 'Why don't we have women deacons?' put in another. The approval was enthusiastic. 'Should we start with one?' asked Bob. 'No', he was told, 'one woman wouldn't speak up in a group of men. We need three women'.

It was decided. At the subsequent church members' meeting an elderly widow, a middle-aged widow and a young married woman were elected as deacons. A little later the men asked why women did not serve at the Communion service. Soon the women were at the Communion table assisting Sue as she conducted the service.

Each year a church meeting was held to decide whether to hold the harvest thanksgiving. No matter how bad the crops had been the answer was always yes. One year a widower, notoriously lazy, proposed that no harvest festival be held. Hardly had he sat down when the oldest woman deacon was on her feet. 'You say no harvest festival this year! Well, you listen. We women do most of the gardening work, don't we? We do the clearing, we do the digging, we do the planting, we do the weeding, we dig up the vegetables, we carry them home. So we are going to say whether we have a harvest festival or not, and we say we are going to have one!' Her proposition was put and carried unanimously.

The women told Sue that when the Gospel was first preached in their district they liked the message and attended the services.

101

Often their husbands did not like them going to church and thrashed them when they got home. They said it happened again and again till in the end their husbands went with them, became Christians and later became the leaders in the church.

With the help of the pastor's wife, Sue started a women's club on Friday afternoons. They sang, had a talk, did some sewing, and finished with games, relay races and perhaps cricket. At first Sue was careful to finish the meetings early so that the women could cook their evening meal, the only big meal of the day. Then the men decided that it was good for the women to have some fun and learn new things. They said they would light the fires and start cooking the evening meal on Fridays.

One thing that was discussed at the meetings was washing houses. If Sue wanted help to wash the church or school there were always plenty of volunteers but they could not see the point of washing their own homes. The houses had to be thatched every four or five years. When the roof was off, the house was washed by the dew or the rain, so they weren't very dirty! Sue and Bob brought up the idea of house washing at church, at school, at the women's club, till at last they felt people were becoming convinced.

They bought in a supply of fairly strong carbolic soap and announced at church one Sunday; 'If you want to wash your house, we will give you a piece of soap at next Friday morning's service'. Though it was women's work, the men offered to carry the water while the women put all their goods out in the street, ready for the scrubbing of the floor. A big congregation turned up and were given their soap and told, 'This afternoon we will come and look at your houses'.

About three o'clock Sue and Bob walked down the hill to the village. It had been a bright, sunny day and blankets and mats were airing in the village street. The people invited the missionaries into their houses, urging them to notice the clean smell and the shiny floors. They were tired but so happy with the result. House-scrubbing became a monthly occurrence and other villages took up the idea.

As they picked their way among the goods outside the houses, Bob would pick up a hammer and say, 'Mine, I think?' The answer was always, 'Yes, of course'. Quite a few tools from the mission station were retrieved that day. The people did not look on it as stealing but if they needed a tool and Sue and Bob were away, they would go to the station and take it. If Bob needed a tool he would ask for it in church or school and it would be returned. The people felt that if the missionaries did not ask for the missing item, they did not need it.

The house was never locked and nothing was ever stolen. When Bob left for a few months' break in Australia during the war, he left some money on his desk. It was still there when he returned!

Seketovo and Vabu Isaako were two women who had a great influence. They were among the first to learn to sing. Before the Gospel came, women did not sing. The men sang songs for the dancing which were very monotonous and not very musical. When the first pastor came from Pari he taught the people the Rarotongan prophet songs in Motu, in which the women sing a separate, high part. These two learnt those 'peroveta songs'. Seketovo had been the wife of a student at Lawes' College, but her husband had died. Later she had married again in Saroa and had a son by each marriage. When Sue met her she was a widow living in Saroa till Sue suggested that the widower Nou Airi marry her!

Nou died in 1939. One Saturday morning after he had died, Seketovo walked up to Saroa to talk to Sue. 'I always take a women's class in Sunday school, and my husband used to go over the lesson with me, to make sure I understood it. The new pastor wants me to keep the class on, so I've come to ask you to help me get the lesson ready'. Sue helped her, she unwillingly accepted a meal and then walked home. Twenty kilometres to prepare a Sunday school lesson! She came each Saturday morning as long as she was able to walk the distance. If Bob was home he would take her back in the truck, but she never asked for a lift.

Seketovo and Vabu Isaako both died in 1946. Born in the days of utter darkness they had come to Christ as young girls and served him all their lives.

There was another woman whose name Sue did not know. As was the custom, she was known by her eldest son's name, 'Bagu's mother'. She was from Ikeaga and had visited many villages with Sue, carrying the missionary's bedroll: a mat, a sheet, a light blanket, a pillow and a mosquito net. She was proud of her four sons. One became a pastor, one a foreman and deacon of Boroko United Church in Port Moresby, one a school teacher, and the youngest a solicitor, the first from those inland villages.

When Sue had retired and was living in Port Moresby, her friend died. Although Bagu sent word to his brother the teacher, he arrived home too late for the funeral. He wrote to Sue:

Sinabada, my mother, your friend, is dead. My brother Bagu wrote and told me so I went home. I went to her grave and sat down. I wept, a bit for me and a bit for you. Then I remembered. She knew the Way of Life and so did my father and they are both with Jesus Christ. Why was I crying? I decided to write you, her friend, a letter.

News of the family, the church and the village followed. Sue was proud to be thought of as his mother's friend.

Polygamy

When Sue arrived in Papua the church rule was that no polygamist could be a church member. He could become an adherent, but not a member able to take part in the Communion service.

Sue accepted that rule until she came to the Saroa district where polygamy, though not frequent, was still present. The Ikeaga people told her that Wala Duma, the first outstanding Christian, had had four wives and the missionary had not told him to do anything but take good care of them. The chief of Karekodobu, the village near Kalaigoro, also had more than one wife. He was not a church member although very helpful to the church.

When Sue moved to Saroa there were no cases of polygamy there and the church was very strong. In one of the Sinaugoro villages lived Gabi Dagaru, who was very anxious to become a full member of the church. Sue asked why he had taken a second wife. He explained that he had been married some years and he and his wife had no children. One day he and his wife talked the matter over and decided that he must take a second wife and if there were children the two wives would share them. So he took a second wife and the two women got on very well together. One son was born and the two women shared him and loved him dearly. They were a truly happy family and all three wanted to join the church.

Sue took the case to the annual committee meeting, asking that this family be allowed to become church members, but was told it was against the rules. She became very angry and asked how she was to explain to her people that when they received Jesus Christ they received life and forgiveness from God. Yet they were still not considered 'good enough' to become church members. The missionaries had no answer and Sue received quite a bit of encouragement from some of the more experienced people. One said that he was sure there was an earlier ruling in the P.D.C. minutes that would allow membership.

A man was allowed to become a village policeman if he had two wives, but if he took a second wife after his appointment, he was sacked. Sue felt that a similar rule should apply in the church. With the help of others she searched through the old P.D.C. minute books and by the following year, had found the old ruling. It said that if a man and his wives lived happily together and all wanted to join the church they should be accepted, but such men could not hold any office.

Permission was given to accept Gabi Dagaru and his wives into the church. The little boy grew to about ten and while the Rankins were on leave he died. His parents said that during his sickness he had comforted them by telling them not to worry about him. He assured them that he knew he was going to be with Jesus. He reminded them that they knew the Way and as long as they were faithful they would all meet again and be happy together. The Good News dramatically changed the way the people met death.

Chapter 13

The walk to Mount Brown

In 1946 Pastor Petero of Wiga was placed in the first village of the Nobone tribe, Bumegoro, a climb of 500 metres from the river. The village was situated on a spur from which steep cliffs dropped away on both sides to the valleys below. The missionaries were preparing for their march into the Mount Brown area.

After the collection meetings, which were held at Gomore that year, the missionaries returned to Saroa to prepare for the patrol to Mount Brown. They called the inland teachers together at Saroa and told them they thought the time had come. These men were full of enthusiasm and excitement. It only involved a small group but this was an adventure into new territory for them as well as for the missionaries. The Mount Brown area was strange and therefore feared.

The area was regularly patrolled by government officers and an aid post with a medical orderly had been opened at Wiga. There was a 'Basileia Dalana', a government road. Now a road of the Kingdom of God was to be made, to bring peace and hope to the people of Mount Brown.

Here is the story of this historic patrol, as written by Sue to her friends in Great Britain and Australia:

We left Saroa on Wednesday 6 August, going by lorry to the Government Plantation at Gobaragere where we spent the night. Next morning we crossed the Kemp Welch River to the new village of Boregaina. We stayed the night and the next morning set off into the hills, going first to Gevera where we slept. Next day being Saturday we set off for Boku, accompanied by a crowd who were going to spend Sunday with us.

Sunday morning, the church was packed and twenty-one adults were baptised. We preached what they called the 'Mount Brown Sermon'. Bob and I preached on marching orders and for the rest of the day answered questions and talked with the leaders and those keen to take part in the trip. We warned them that it would probably cost a lot in hardship and so we must move carefully and slowly, thinking out each step of the way. We made it clear that the aim of this first trip would be to make friends.

Monday we spent examining the school, baking bread, washing and ironing clothes. We left for Wiga on Tuesday morning and the Boku church folks insisted on carrying me so that I wouldn't get tired too early on! For the first time the Boku men refused to accept payment for carrying our goods. That was because the teacher there was an Ikeaga man, and the Ikeaga people always carried our goods for the love of the work.

At Wiga we held a council of war. Mamata came from Ikeaga and brought some of his deacons and lay readers. There were many questions. Which way should we go and which way should we return? How long would it take? Could we be certain of getting food or had we better take supplies?

Only two men with us seemed to know anything about the way, and what they said didn't agree. We decided, after much talk, to go and return the same way. We took the advice of Diuga, the lay reader from Wiga, who said we would get plenty of food. He said the Mount Brown people had promised him. So we decided to take only what was necessary for our two selves and tobacco and salt to pay for food for the carriers and the rest of the group.

It was really an invasion of the new area by Christians. We were joined early next morning by men from the three Ikeaga villages. There were eight boys from the Saroa station and Pastor John from Boku. We collected others on the way. It was like a small army. After prayers and a short charge from Mamata, we started off. Our companions were like children going to a picnic, full of high spirits and expectation.

The weather was lovely — dry and not too hot — so we made good progress. We passed through one Wiga village and there were people waiting for us with food cooked ready for our followers and huge pieces of sugarcane. After a rest while the men polished off the eats, we went on again and much sooner than we expected we came in sight of our new centre at Bumegoro, the centre for the Nobone villages, where Petero had opened up work the previous year.

Long before we reached the village we could hear the people singing and when we got there we were amazed at the number present. The Nobone people had declared a holiday and come in from all six villages to see us and join in the new venture. Bumegoro was a lovely spot and the teacher's house was very comfortable. They provided us with our own small dining room and bedroom and a room to use as a bathroom, with a dish and a bucket of hot water. We bathed by pouring the water over us and allowing it to run away between the rough floor timbers.

That afternoon we talked to the people and played with the children, getting to know them all. My watch came in very useful. The little ones loved to come and hear its 'sek, sek' not 'tick, tick'. In the evening we had a sing-song and our school boys from Saroa gave a demonstration of Kiwai dancing which gave much pleasure. After prayers at ten o'clock we went to bed in a nice clean room with mats on the floor. We appreciated it still more when we returned to it!

Next morning, a short service and then off. We were such a crowd. Most of the able-bodied men from the Nobone villages went with us.

We were now in the haunts of the bird of paradise and the women used the call whenever they wanted to show pleasure. They put their hands above their heads and gave the call over and over again. It was musical and most effective. When I walked over to the women and joined in, it brought the house down. The women saw us off with their bird calls till we could no longer see or hear them.

The track at first was good but soon we began to climb and then we came to a big hill where the track led along the steep side, only about six inches wide and at an angle. After an hour or so of walking in the same position the calf of my left leg began to ache like fury and I wondered whether I would be able to keep going. Then we went down again. The annoying part about those hills was that after getting right to the top on one side we had to go to the very bottom on the other side and then start all over again. All that day we walked up hill and down except that occasionally we walked along the side of the mountain instead.

About midday we came to a small village called Senemaka, the end of the Nobone country and the beginning of the Mount Brown area. The people cooked food for us and gave us sugarcane. Bob and I had a cup of tea and a short rest. There we made the acquaintance of Otaba, the village policeman, who was very keen to help us. He was used to recruiting unwilling carriers for the patrol officers and had a line of men from his village ready to go with us. He was pushing and shoving and shouting at them. I said through Pastor John who was the interpreter, 'Tell him not to touch the men. If they don't want to go, good. If they do want to go, good, but he is not to touch them'. When John told him he couldn't believe it. He said, 'Can't I go?' John said, 'Yes, you can go, but you are not to bump or push anyone. They are only to go if they want to'. Then he understood the missionaries' way of working and became our guide for the next part of our journey.

After another two hours of the same type of walking, we came near to the first Mount Brown villages. They were on the hilltops and out of our way, but as we entered a wooded area we found people from those villages waiting for us and the women busy with stone ovens cooking food for us. So we sat down and enjoyed the food, but we were stumped. The people didn't know Motu or Sinaugoro and we didn't know their language. Diuga and Otaba knew a smattering. We shook hands, said, 'Buni' (good) and tried to talk with the help of those who knew a little Motu.

We found that in the Mount Brown villages all the cooking was done in stone ovens. Pits were dug and filled with firewood and stones to be heated. Then the

108

food was wrapped in leaves and placed between layers of hot stones. The food took a couple of hours to cook.

How I wished I could talk to those people! We gave the children a lolly and then we had to leave them. We still had a long way to go.

The men wanted to carry me. I let them carry me in the safe spots, which were few. I felt much safer on my own feet in the steep places. If I had been dropped it was a very long way to fall.

We came to places where the trees and bushes were covered with moss. We were very high up in the mountains. In places we were following the Bima River towards its source. Again the track led us up and then down, but mostly up. About 4.30 p.m. we reached Boko village with fourteen houses. The people fed us with vegetables and sugarcane. The sugarcane was so juicy and refreshing. There were no coconut palms at such an altitude and the schoolboys became very tired of the dry baked foods. We missed the young coconuts which are so thirst-quenching.

The houses were very small and to our eyes, used to the large thatched houses of the Sinaugoro people, very poor buildings. There seemed to be more than one family to a house, for we often saw four adults on one small veranda. Some houses had no veranda, but just one small room.

We talked to the people, again through the interpreters, and tried to make friends, gave salt in exchange for food, and a lolly to each child and went on. The men said we must hurry to get to our camp before dark. We reached one more village whence we had a good view of Mount Brown (Bima) just for a few minutes. It didn't deign to show itself much; clouds and mist veiled the peak most of the time. We talked to the people and then went off to the camp on the river bank. It was the rest house built for the use of government officers. We arrived just before dark. A few minutes later men came along with fish and our companions were delighted. They put on a billy.

Then we heard drumming and into the little light that was left came a band of dancers. Soon another group joined them, men and women, boys and girls. Fires were lit and we could see more clearly as they danced up and down for us. Instead of the headdresses high in front that we were used to, these had only teeth (cuscus, a type of large possum, or tree kangaroo teeth) and cuscus fur on their foreheads, but hanging down their backs were plumes made of cassowary feathers and whole birds of paradise mounted on cane. It wasn't long before one of the men took off his headdress for me to inspect. The plumes jiggled up and down as they danced.

Some men had pigtails tied tightly with bark. Up to four or five pigtails were worn, tied together at the ends. When we asked the meaning of the pigtails we were told two reasons: that they were done specially for the dance and that they were a sign of mourning. After their welcome we had prayers about 9 p.m. and went to bed. The dancers went back to the village and continued their celebration.

In the morning came our first hitch. Some of our large company wanted to turn back. They said they were hungry and we could expect no more food as there were no more villages near the track. We called Mamata, our senior teacher, and asked his advice. 'Go on, even if we do suffer hunger,' he said. Then we asked our schoolboys. 'If we go back from here people will laugh at us,' they said. Those were our sentiments, too, so we called the folks together and said that we were going on, but that those who had doubts had better go back. No-one went.

After about four hours of tramping we came to a second camp and there were people waiting for us with the ovens steaming away. In the early afternoon we set off on the last lap to the village of Sanomu, the end of the Rigo section of the Mount Brown area. Mount Brown men carried our goods. Before starting they gave us their 'college yell', quite the most musical one we had heard. Every now and again on the way they stopped and repeated the performance, to our joy.

It was not very far, but a steady climb. In places we had to clutch hold of roots and small shrubs to help us. When we reached the camp there again were the people and more ovens steaming. It sounds as though our companions were over-fed, but we were so many that when shared out, the rations were far from large. The camp was on the spur of a hill while the village itself was on the top and in the background Mount Brown wreathed itself in clouds and mist.

I went to the women and tried to talk to them. Fortunately there were some youths who had been away working and so knew a little Motu and they came to our rescue. The women let me hold their babies and the wee things weren't scared. I told them via the youths that I had a boy, and there was much chatter and then the questions were put to me. How big was he? Where was he? Why didn't I bring him? When would he come? That was something in common and the ice was broken.

A coterie of small boys gathered wherever I went, and there it was the same. I had with me two small chaps from Bumegoro, the teacher's small son and his pal. They had kept up with me all the way and had carried a small bag for about half the distance. When the other little boys saw that they had no fear of me they began to come round and chatter. Then the rain came and there was an exodus, for with the rain came a very cold wind which blew in great gusts down from Mount Brown, looming in the background.

We went to the rest house, got washed and changed, made our beds, got an evening meal and finally had prayers. There was only one smallish house for us all so it was more than a squash. Fifteen of us got into that one room, while others stayed under the house with fires and blankets. But the cold gusts of wind made them very miserable.

Sunday dawned bright and clear and when the sun warmed us we all felt happier. We held our own service on the hill, dedicating ourselves to the work of that day and to making friends with the people. One of the hymns we sang that morning was Jesus shall reign. We felt that to bring that reign among those hill people would be really worthwhile.

We had no food supplies so the prayer, 'Give us this day our daily bread,' had new meaning for us. Hardly had the prayer ended when women started coming down the hill with bags of vegetables. Fires were soon lit, some vegetables were cooked in the ashes but most went into the stone ovens. But stones take a while to get hot. When the food was put in the ovens we gathered the people together for a service. An ex-member of the armed constabulary offered to interpret for me, and he seemed to do it fairly well, prompted by two or three others who supplied what he left out.

After the service we went up to the village and talked as best we could with the people, specially the women and old men. The women wore skirts made from broad leaves which they had split and dried. The men wore 'sihis', a twenty centimetre wide strip of tapa cloth, hammered from bark. They wound it round their waists in a broad belt and between their legs. We saw such a lot of old men in those villages. They looked like Australian Aborigines with their wrinkled foreheads, thick-set bodies and beards.

One old gent said he'd like to offer me a smoke from his pipe. I explained that I didn't smoke and asked him to excuse me. I'm not at all sure what the implications of accepting a smoke from him would have been!

We went into some of their houses. The people had woven mats to hang on the walls to keep out the wind. We also saw their store houses. These were long, narrow houses built on very slender piles, and each family was allotted a room for their yams. In Sanomu there were four such houses. Their own homes are not big enough to take people, dogs and food.

From the village we could see ten other Mount Brown villages on the hills and slopes around. In between Sanomu and Senemaka were six other villages, making seventeen in all.

Our men asked us if we could go back to the last camp to sleep that night because it was too cold for them at Sanomu. We agreed and set off down the hill. The Sanomu people seemed quite upset and the women followed us down the hill, calling after us with their beautiful bird of paradise call.

We had seen very few older children, though there had been lots of small ones and babies. On the way down we asked Mamata. He said, 'Oh, they've sent them off into the bush to hide, because they are afraid we might take them away'. He went on to explain that when the missionaries first came to his village his father sent him into the bush and also told him that if he met a missionary and he said anything about 'school' he must pretend to be 'not all there'.

Just as we arrived at the lower camp by the river, rain began to fall and the people started to pour out of the bush from all directions. They had come from all the villages round Sanomu to meet us. This time there were big children. The fear was going. In a short time the women had fires going and peeled the vegetables and heated up the stones. Our schoolboys who were tired of such dry food, begged raw vegetables and boiled them.

'While the food was cooking, our schoolboys sang for the people and then the other villages with us took turns and kept it up till about ten p.m. when we had prayers and turned in. My watch and torch had been busy all evening and I was surrounded by small boys and girls. They were quite the friendliest children I have come across in Papua. They just took possession of me, held my hands, stroked my arms, rubbed their faces up and down my arms and at last two boys just pulled my arms around their necks. We couldn't talk but we got on all right.

Presently I went to sit on the steps of the rest house, so my escort followed me and sat beside me and we played with the torch.

I did know a word or two of the Mount Brown language by this time, for I took down some words from the youths and old men and the few words I said brought such smiles. Next morning we had prayers, talked to them, told them about our work, asked if when they got to know us they would let four boys come and live with us. Some of the boys wanted to come right away but we didn't think that was wise.

One young man said he wanted to come to Saroa and learn our Way. He went to get his wife and when he didn't reappear, we thought it had just been talk. A fortnight after our return to Saroa he turned up to say that his wife was somewhat scared so they wanted to stay with our teacher at Bumegoro till Christmas and learn a little of the Way from the teacher first.

We were sorry to turn and leave Mount Brown but the return journey was easier and we got back to Bumegoro very quickly. Full of joy, we spent the evening telling the story of what we had found. Then to Wiga and on to Ikeaga. At Ikeaga we found that only two old men had been left behind in the village nearest the teacher's station. All the able-bodied men had gone with us.

The women had made a song and taught it to the children. Long before we could see them we heard the women singing, and they sang while we climbed the hill to the village. The men were really thrilled because their women had made a song. When we arrived at the teacher's house the children were all there singing:

> The shepherds of the sheep are arriving.
> Who are they? This is who they are:
> Gentle people who come in no other name
> But in the Name of Jesus Christ.
> We see them. We rejoice. (Three times)
> In no other name
> But in the Name of Jesus Christ. Rejoice!

Next morning in their church we had a huge congregation, much too large to get into the building. They had come from many nearby villages. There were forty-one people to be baptised. What a climax to the adventure. Prayers of thanks were given for our safe return and we knew that in all our churches, from Gabagaba to the inland, people had been praying for our safety. Thus they all had a share in the venture.

Those who went with us thanked us over and over again because, owing to us, they had at last been to that dreaded part, Mount Brown, and found that it was like their own part of the country and the people like themselves.

Before we left Ikeaga we discussed what we should do next and we decided that for the next year or so we must keep in touch and strengthen the bonds of friendship. We would not put a teacher in till the people asked for one and showed definite interest in the Christian Way. So we returned to Saroa three weeks after we left. Physically it had been hard going but well worth it.

Chapter 14

New developments

Almost immediately after that first visit, the people of those Mount Brown villages began giving money to get the work started. There was quite a lot of visiting done by the pastors from the other villages and their church members, and the Mount Brown folks were welcomed into the other villages whenever they were passing through on their way to the Government Station at Rigo.

The 1948 collection meetings were held at Saroa. There was not enough food or money to feed several hundred people for a week. It was suggested that only teachers and deacons or representatives come to the meetings. But the Saroa deacons arranged all the hospitality and in spite of the missionaries' request, crowds of people came, specially from Nobone and Mount Brown. The Nobone teacher explained that they were so keen on coming that he could not stop them. The evening before the collection meeting they brought their contribution to Bob, one hundred and two pounds (two hundred and four dollars).

At the meeting the next day the missionaries held the Mount Brown contribution till last. Gabagaba, which always led in the contributions, gave one hundred and one pounds and thought they had again been the top givers. They found they were outdone by the newest part of the district. Everyone was delighted at the generosity of the inlanders and gratified to know that they wanted teachers. Each of the Mount Brown villages and Nobone village had given sums ranging from two pounds to eighteen pounds.

113

The Government Patrol Officer returned from a trip to Mount Brown and told Bob and Sue of the beautiful site the people had chosen for their first mission house. The missionaries were praying for the right man to send, one who could work in such an isolated spot.

They were besieged by Mount Brown people asking for a teacher. Several villages had combined to form a larger centre called Gorugoro. Bob and Sue decided to ask Romena Mairi and his wife, who were working in the Delena district, if they were willing to work in Mount Brown. They wrote to Percy Chatterton, asking him to talk the matter over with Romena and Lucy. A radio reply came to say that they were willing to go as pioneers. This village was a day's walk beyond Bumegoro.

While Bob and Sue were having some leave, Romena returned and settled in to his home village of Saroa to await their return. When they arrived they found that Petero at Bumegoro had T.B. and needed treatment. They decided to place Romena and Lucy at Bumegoro. While the Rankins were away Romena had made several visits to Mount Brown. On one occasion he found an epidemic raging and was able to get help quickly. A medical patrol was sent out but the number of deaths was high. When the medical patrol reached the river they could not cross because it was flooded. Romena swam across the flooded river and took the medicines back to his people.

As a result of the epidemic and a dispute with the Government Officer, the village of Gorugoro again split up into two small hamlets. So it was more convenient for Romena to go to Bumegoro to replace Petero and reach into the Mount Brown area from there.

In 1952 the Rev. Bill Bache and his wife Vi who had just arrived in Papua, came to Saroa for a few months. Bill accompanied Bob and Sue on an inland patrol. The stories they had heard of an epidemic with a high death rate were confirmed. At Doromu they found two villages instead of four. The missionaries walked through one deserted village of fourteen houses where drums, nets, and spears were still standing on the verandas. The Doromu people said that all except one elderly couple, one young couple, four widows and a few children had died during the epidemic earlier in the year.

Usually a group of carriers would accompany the missionaries up into the mountains and back again on their inland patrols. Sometimes they went part of the way and then changed over. On one patrol, the Rankins came to a village where they could not persuade anyone to carry for them. Bob and Sue sat and patiently talked to the people till at last the story came out.

There was a blood feud between that village and the next. A young man from the next village had married a girl from their village and lived there. One day in a pig hunt the young man was killed. His relations said that the man had been murdered. The village people insisted that it was an accident.

The Rankins walked on to the next village and talked to the people. They succeeded in making peace, persuading the people to accept the word of the other village. When they returned to Saroa, Bob went to see the District Officer and report the matter to him. The officer was a wise young man. He sent for the men of both villages, talked to them and heard their assurance that the feud was over. Then he gave food to each party, saying that they were to cook it and then bring it to him. When they brought the food he told them to give the food to the opposite group and sit down together and eat. They did, proving that they truly had been reconciled.

First pastors to Mount Brown

In 1953 Pastor Vanere Babona became the first pastor to live in the Mount Brown area. His father, Babona, had been a pastor in the Saroa-Boku district when Sue had arrived.

Vanere and his family were welcomed enthusiastically. Three villages had moved close together on the banks of a small river. The people had built a house and made a garden.

The following year when Sue and Bob arrived at Marunomu with the Rev. Norman Cocks they found a big change. They were welcomed by the schoolchildren, singing. Vanere and family were not living in a Mount Brown-type house but in a strong, well-built dwelling. Vanere, who had trained as a carpenter, had taught the men how to adze timber and build strongly. Vanere and the village men had walked many kilometres to cut grass to thatch the house in the Sinaugoro manner.

The missionaries found that Vanere was holding a reading class for adults at 6 a.m. each day as well as the children's school later in the day.

Remembering their previous visit to Mount Brown, Sue and Bob had told Mr Cocks of the unusual headdresses the people wore. But the people did not come out to dance and when asked to dance for their visitor from Australia they did not wear the headdresses. Sue asked why. They told her that when they moved to Marunomu they had decided they would start a new way and not take any of their old things with them. Some they had sold, some they had given away and some they had burned.

A group of men came to Marunomu from further into Mount Brown territory. They told the missionaries that people from five more Mount Brown villages were waiting at Omenomu to meet them.

When the missionaries continued their walk to Omenomu the men and women pleaded with them. If they moved from the small hamlets on the tops of the mountains and came together at Omenomu, could they have a teacher?

The area was exploding into growth. Other groups of villages were requesting teachers. When asked why they wanted a teacher, the answer was usually, 'We want to learn the Christian Way and we want our children to learn new ways'.

Sue and Bob took stock of their staff and saw no hope of sending a pastor to Omenomu quickly. When they returned to Saroa the Rankins received a letter from Romena at Bumegoro. 'Twenty-six more people have come forward to be baptised. I feel things are moving, the Christian church in Papua is growing', he said.

The people from Omenomu kept coming to Saroa saying, 'Where is our teacher? Can we take him home now?' At last the missionaries asked the Wiga and Ikeaga teachers to call for a volunteer at their local union meeting, the meeting of the churches in their area. A young Wiga man came foward and a group of inland teachers and their people went to Omenomu to induct Emudu as Lay Reader.

Soon after, a large group of men and boys and a few women and girls from Mount Brown came down to the annual collection meetings. The Marunomu people acted the story of the coming of the first white man, a government officer, to their village during World War I. They did it well and realistically, to the hilarious enjoyment of the spectators. There was a breathtaking moment when the chief, tearing round in a frenzy, hurled his spear into the ground right in front of Sue, within six inches of her foot. When the folks realised that she had not been hurt there was a big sigh of relief and then a roar of laughter.

Sue had been working in the Saroa-Boku district for twenty-six years. Although they had been provided with a station waggon for travel between the river and the coast both she and Bob, in their late fifties, were finding the frequent expeditions into the mountains very difficult. They requested that a younger man replace them.

A few years earlier Bob had been asked by P.D.C. to visit Veiru, a mission station near Kikori in the Gulf District which had been set up as a boys' technical school in 1951. The venture had proved too expensive and the school closed. It was suggested that a Bible School be established with a lower entrance standard than Lawes' College, where couples could be taught in Motu. Bob and Sue caught the vision. It would meet the desperate need for more pastors and also fill a pastoral role to the villages tucked away in the swampy backwaters round Veiru.

P.D.C. saw that it would be an appointment where Bob's carpentry skills and business ability could be used to the full in rebuilding the campus, and Sue's teaching skills would come to the fore in designing a course and presiding in the lecture room.

Meanwhile the Rankins were being made aware of the needs of the Barai area which lay between the Mount Brown villages and the Port Moresby mission district. Pastor Tanu Gware and two Lawes' College students had visited the area and returned burdened with the darkness of the people. The patrol officers found the people indifferent and lethargic and in great need of medical care.

With the encouragement of the government officer, the people made the decision to leave their small scattered villages and set up a community on the banks of the Mimani River which was towards the head-waters of the Kemp Welch. They called the centre Dorobisoro.

Then, at last, some men came down to Saroa to ask for a teacher. Prayers were being answered. The men were told to go home, build a house and make a garden for their pastor and come back to Saroa when all was ready. Sue and Bob were away at P.D.C. when the men arrived. When they could not find the missionaries they went to talk to the government officer. He assured them that the Rankins always kept their word and advised them to go up to the river to wait. When they heard that the missionaries had returned they came down to Saroa.

Caught napping, Sue and Bob had no-one to send. They did not believe in just telling someone to go. It was a very primitive inland area and very difficult for a man from the coast to adjust to the cold weather and strange food; almost more difficult for a Papuan from the coast than for an expatriate because there was great fear of traditional enemies and of sorcery and magic.

However, it was time for the annual pastors' meetings in 1955. The missionaries told the pastors of the need at Dorobisoro and asked if one of them would be willing to go. There was no response and they were very troubled at having to disappoint the Barai people. But later on the Saturday night Tom Nou, a young Port Moresby man who was pastor at Tauruba, came and said that he and his wife, Geua, would like to go to the Barai.

Tom's father, Pastor Nou Aire of Pari village, had gone as a volunteer to help Sue at Kalaigoro in 1930. Tom grew up there but later went to the Port Moresby mission station as a boarder. He decided to train as a pastor and went to Lawes' College. When he graduated Tom asked to work in the Saroa district. He went to Tauruba which had been a difficult place to work but in 1955 Sue wrote:

Now there is a strong group there (Tauruba), the leaders of the village are sympathetic, the children are attending school regularly and the whole tone of the village is friendly. From 1951 this group of villages had teachers from the Port Moresby district. They did a good job and Tauruba changed from being a 'pain in the neck' to a village with a strong school and a strong church fellowship.

Tom was chairman of Torchbearers, the L.M.S. youth organisation, for the Saroa district that year. When Bob announced at the Torchbearers rally the next day that Tom had volunteered to go to Dorobisoro, the young people were very proud and excited. At the same meeting Tom's father, Nou Aire, was honoured as he completed his ministry and prepared to return to Pari to retire.

In his 1955 report Bob Rankin writes that in opening up the Barai centres they had more or less rounded off the inland work which he and his wife had been aiming towards opening since the end of World War II. He describes how it was now possible to make a round trip to the Mount Brown villages via Wiga and Bumegoro and then to continue to the Barai and return to the Kemp Welch via Doromu. But he also reports that more villages of the Mount Brown language group further east, north of Abau, wanted to move into larger communities so that the Saroa district could send them a pastor. He continues; 'There are everywhere pockets of country still untouched, while even some old established places have at present no teachers. The call comes to us from all those places as it did to Paul at Troas, "Come over and help us".' To the Rankins' evangelists' hearts there was nothing more painful than having to say, 'We have no-one to send'.

In June 1956, the Rev. Laurie Gray, who was to become the new Saroa district missionary, arrived from Sydney. It was planned that he work with the Rankins till the end of the year and Sue would teach him Motu. Then the senior missionaries would take leave in Great Britain for one year before returning in 1958 to open Chalmers College at Veiru.

118

Chapter 15

A year of goodbyes

The mission station was being invaded by hundreds of people from the mountains on their way to Ginigolo Gunugau for the annual collection meetings. Before the missionaries set out for the gathering at the twin villages near Vatorata, Bob and Laurie spent two days counting the collection money. Two thousand pounds was given for the support of pastors and maintenance of buildings.

Meanwhile Sue ministered to the long line of people who arrived each day for medical care. As Laurie took note of his duties as district minister he was overwhelmed at the sight of so many tropical ulcers, boils, infected sores and cuts. By this year the Rankins were using the wonder drug penicillin which quickly healed many of the infections. Babies and old people with ulcers exposing the bone, cases of malaria, yaws, the ever present skin disease and scabies were all treated during those hectic few days before the missionaries drove down to Rigo and then walked up the track to the host villages for the collection meetings.

Sue was carried on a chair on poles in the midst of a crowd of about a hundred people to her last annual meetings in the Saroa district. After an hour, as the group came to the entrance to the villages, they were welcomed by a crowd of several hundred, the men dressed in bright headdresses made of fur, and feathers from cockatoos, cassowaries, pigeons and birds of paradise. Their faces were painted and round their necks were strings of dogs' teeth, sharks' teeth and boars' tusks. The men wore sihis of tapa cloth and the women grass skirts.

After shaking hands with the chief, the councillors, the policemen and hundreds of others the missionaries were shown the house built specially for their use during the meetings. Although there were only eight church members in the two villages, the entire population had taken part in raising the money for the collection (250 pounds) and to entertain their guests (150 pounds). It was a matter of pride to all the villagers that their guests be well cared for.

Sue was feeling very deeply the impending parting with the people she loved so much. She found displays of emotion painful and knew that the people were feeling they could not continue without her. She determined to focus the people's eyes on the future and the welcome to the new missionary and to avoid long, emotional farewells. Therefore she and Bob planned an inland patrol on which they would say their goodbyes but also introduce their new colleague.

In August the three set out on the Rankins' first visit to the Barai. In five weeks they planned to show Laurie as much of the inland part of the district as possible. Just as they were leaving, Pastor Reatau Mea of Port Moresby, chairman of the Papua Church Assembly, arrived to visit the district. After visiting the coastal villages he was invited to join the inland patrol. The party travelled to the river on a truck owned by one of the Saroa village men. Laurie had his first sight of the Kemp Welch River and the rubber and coconut plantations on its banks.

That night the party slept in the rest house at Gobakigolo. It was a heathen village, the people dirty and needing medical care. One baby had a huge ulcer on its stomach. Knowing that it needed a few days' treatment, Sue suggested that the father accompany them to Ikeaga. When he refused, she threatened to report him to the government officer at Rigo because the child would die without treatment. That had the desired effect.

Walking downhill through grasslands and forest the party came to a wide stream of beautiful clear water, gleaming and shimmering in the sunlight. On the opposite bank were some of the Ikeaga people waiting to welcome them with food prepared. During the 300 metre climb to the village, people lined the path to greet the party and sing a song they had composed for the Rankins' departure. As the crowd walked up the hill they sang: 'This is the last time that you will have joy with us'. After taking part in a farewell service Pastor Reatau and his companions returned to the coast while the rest of the party continued to Wiga and Bumegoro.

Romena had levelled the ground round his house, which was large and well-built, and had planted flowering trees. Many of the men who carried Sue were the sons of the young men who had patrolled with Sue and Becky thirty years before. The road after Bumegoro wound along the side of a steep hill. It was one of those places where Sue preferred to walk, just wide enough to put one foot in front of the other. Finally her legs would not carry her any longer. She sat on a log, feeling she could not move.

Bob and the carriers had gone ahead so Laurie went on to tell them Sue needed help. In the meantime she recovered enough to limp to a clearing where the others were boiling the billy. Pastor Mamata, who had already retired, accompanied his beloved missionaries all the way. They thought it would be too much for him but he said he wanted to go with them so that when they were hungry he, too, would be hungry, when they were tired, he, too, would be tired, when they were thirsty, he, too, would be thirsty. That evening Sue sat beside Mamata. He asked how she felt. 'All right except for my knees,' she replied. He answered, 'Yes, mine are aching, too'.

At Marunomu and Omenomu Sue and Bob were delighted to hear how the Mount Brown people had learned to sing and took great pleasure in the lovely, resonant, bird calls they gave. They were amazed to see the size of the schools. At Omenomu, Emudu was struggling with 111 children. It was a cold place, the houses were small and built very close to the river. A large crowd came to the Sunday morning service which Romena conducted in Police Motu. About 130 children packed onto a veranda to listen to Vanere telling the story of David and Goliath.

From Omenomu the track was long and difficult, climbing to over 1000 metres, then down a long hill to the Ormond River at 300 metres. A muddy walk along the river was followed by another long climb. Badaiika village was built on a ridge. The verandas of the houses were at ground level but the posts at the back of each house were very, very long. As Sue was leaning out of the back window of the pastor's house cleaning her teeth, she dropped her dentures. As Laurie and Bob clambered down the side of the hill to retrieve them Sue saw the humour of the situation but Bob was not amused.

From Mount Brown the party headed for the Barai area close to the top of the Owen Stanley Range, passing close to the spirit mountain called the Baron or Durigolo. Sue writes:

We walked through moss forests of huge trees, too big to cut down. My walking stick sank right down into the moss. It was very quiet, like walking on thick carpet. The constant dripping of the rain made it a bit dreary but the trees were magnificent, laden with moss. It was very hard walking and a very stiff climb to the first Barai village. As we were leaning against a tree trying to get our

121

breath, one of the men said to me, 'This hill is a bloody bastard'. It was the only description possible.

In one place we had to walk down a very rough little creek. I asked its name and they said, 'Sorry'. Thinking it unusual I asked the reason. The men said that during the war they had carried wounded soldiers over the Owen Stanleys and down that track. It was so rough that they could not avoid bumping them, so they were always saying, 'Sorry!' I was very touched by that story of the compassion of the Papuan men.

They rested at Tabu and the people fed them delicious purple yams. It should have been a two-day walk to Dorobisoro, but Tom Nou wanted them to be there for Sunday, so the weary party went on their way. As they descended to the Mimani River they caught sight of the village, not far to go now. Then the welcome began. Barai men in full warpaint rushed at the missionaries with spears poised to throw, then stopped short and laughed and welcomed them. Everyone trooped across the suspension bridge to the house that Tom had built.

Tied to the veranda rails were dozens of long yams, each painted with a face. The house was very roomy and after spending three nights in rest houses Bob, Sue and Laurie were delighted to see a bathroom with plenty of water. Tom's home had become the community centre of the village and school and on Sunday morning more than two hundred people gathered under it for the church service. No-one in the party knew that Barai language and communication was rather slow in Motu.

There were many people with dreadful sores which horrified the schoolboys from Saroa. They were amazed when Sue told them that when she first went to Saroa it was just the same there. A young man had accompanied Tom and was helping him with the school of 114 children. Sue and Bob felt that the work of bringing the Gospel and a new way of life to the Barai people had been well started. Tom and his family had been living in Dorobisoro a short five months. The pastor told how the chief had come to him on his arrival and said, 'See this spear! If you don't get out of here quickly I will use it to kill you'. When asked what Tom had done, he quietly said; 'That man was the first to become a Christian'.

The party spent a couple of days getting to know the people. Among them they found some visitors from the north side of the range which was cared for by the Anglican mission. They begged the missionaries to send them a teacher, too. It was the new missionary's first experience of the pain of having to say that no-one was available. He was so aware that Christ had met his need for salvation and of the look of hopelessness on the men's faces as they turned away.

The river by the village was very beautiful, fast flowing over cascades and small falls. The vivid crimson D'Albertis creeper festooned the trees and small orchids bloomed in the trees and crevices in the rocks.

The road from the Barai down to the Kemp Welch River was narrow, steep and slippery. It was tough going for Sue and Bob, with constant climbing and descending for four days. Each night the party slept in rest houses as there were few villages and most of them were Seventh Day Adventist. As they travelled down, the river became faster and wider till at last the carriers were able to make rafts and the missionaries floated down to Dirinomu.

In spite of being very tired, the Rankins then took their new colleague to Boku and a few of the river villages. The people pleaded with the Rankins; 'Jesus stayed with his disciples, please stay with us'. Sue gently reminded them that the Lord had said that it was better that he should leave them. She and Bob explained that it was better that they leave because they were getting too old to climb the hills. They then objected that the new man could not possibly love them as the Rankins had. Laurie assured the people that he already loved them.

The group arrived at Kokebagu looking forward to a night of the hospitality of their friends the Brownlies, but Bob was feeling ill. Sue asked Grace Brownlie, who was a trained nurse, to look at his eyes. They were very jaundiced. It was essential to get Bob to hospital. Peter Brownlie brought the truck to the door and the party returned to Saroa. Leaving Laurie in charge of the station, Sue and Bob went to Gabagaba to find a boat bound for Port Moresby.

After a stay in hospital with hepatitis for Bob, he and Sue returned to Saroa to say their last farewells. When Sue told the people that Bob had recovered much quicker than was usual from his illness they said, 'Of course, weren't we all praying for him, from Gabagaba to Mount Brown?'

Policeman Otabu came to see his friends. He was very upset. He had been to the government station and had been told that he was too old for the policeman's job. The government officer had taken his uniform, a dark blue serge laplap which was very warm, and sent him off in a shirt and a pair of shorts. He said to Sue, 'Sinabada, will you please tell the King of Britain what they've done to the King of the Gunika (inland)?' Sue's son, Bob, who was spending their last few days at Saroa with his parents, gave Otabu a warm pullover. Bob senior went to see the government officer. 'You were a bit hard on the old chap,' he said. 'Oh, he's too old,' replied the officer. Bob said, 'Yes, but surely you could have let him keep his uniform, after all those years of service. You hurt his dignity'. He said, 'Oh, I'm sorry', and sent for the old fellow and gave him back his uniform.

The people of Saroa collected forty pounds as a gift to the Rankins. They came to Sue and Bob and said, 'We have a gift for you but we are not going to give it to you because you will just put it back into the work. We are going to send two men to Port Moresby with you and they will buy what you choose for yourselves'. The Rankins chose a typewriter. The people of Gabagaba and the Saroa district people working in Port Moresby also sent farewell gifts to their friends.

After a year's leave in Great Britain, February 1958 saw the Rankins boarding a catalina of wartime vintage in Port Moresby harbour for the flight to their new home near Kikori.

Chapter 16

To the gulf district

The passengers followed a motley collection of mailbags, freezer boxes, and luggage into the cabin. Seated in the side-saddle aluminium seats, they turned and watched through the small windows as Port Moresby fell away below them. 'Enjoy the sunshine and blue sea while you can', joked one of the passengers, 'Kikori is mostly mud and rain'.

After calling at Kerema, Bob and Sue stood in the perspex bubble of the aircraft watching the swamps of the delta spread out below them. Dark green vegetation was intersected by thousands of waterways, some large estuaries penetrating from the ocean into the swamp, others so narrow that they were almost obscured by the vast covering of mangroves. Columns of vapour rose unwaveringly into the steamy atmosphere.

'That is Aird Hills', Bob said, indicating the only feature to break the monotony of the delta landscape. Sue could see a group of buildings on the side of one of the hills and two large villages spread along the river bank. Aird Hills was the headstation of the Delta district of the L.M.S., established by the Rev. Ben Butcher after James Chalmers and Oliver Tomkins were killed and eaten on Goaribari Island at the mouth of the Kikori River in 1901.

The catalina descended rapidly between the wooded banks of the Kikori River. As the plane touched down, two sea anchors thrown out from the bubble acted as brakes, allowing the pilot to taxi gently up to the landing stage anchored in the river.

The Rev. John Cribb, a lanky Queenslander who was the district missionary, waited on the pontoon to welcome the Rankins and help them transfer their bags into a canoe and across to the *Tamate*, an eleven-metre workboat called by the Papuan name for Chalmers. Standing on the deck the Rankins could see the Kikori government station buildings dotted above the steep river bank and a little further downstream the tradestore with several fragile-looking dugout canoes tied to the wharf. The river was thick, muddy, and brown. The outgoing tide combined with the current to carry the *Tamate* along at more than her accustomed eight knots.

A few kilometres down stream from Kikori, Veiru was situated on one of the few pieces of solid ground in the delta; one hundred acres bounded by the Kikori River, Tipeiewo Creek, and the swamp. John Cribb indicated a large waterway flowing into the Kikori on the left. 'Aird Hills is about ten kilometres down there', he said.

The Papuan and South Sea pastors who had been helping John prepare Veiru for its new role as a Bible College crowded round to welcome the new arrivals and escort them up the steps cut into the river bank and along the path to the house. It was very large, on two metre posts, the thatched roof rising to six metres at the ridge. Under the house was the very necessary area for a tool shed, class-room and space for drying clothes. A wide ditch had been dug round the house under the eaves to carry away some of the 750 millimetres of rain that could be expected each year.

Standing on the landing by the front door of their new home, the Rankins looked out towards the river across vividly green lawns flanked by oil nut palms. Within a few months Sue had planted gardenias and orange ixora along the path to the wharf, and an allamanda was twining its golden blooms and dark glossy leaves around the railing by the front door. In Sue's words:

After lunch on the day of our arrival, John and the pastors showed us the houses they had prepared for the eleven student families who were to arrive within a few days. Bob was full of plans for improving the accommodation and building a lecture hall-cum-church with a library underneath it. I could scarcely wait to start teaching those men and women, preparing them for their work for God as pastors. I could picture them reaching far into the most primitive villages of Papua with the healing message of God's Light and Love.

The pastors went back to their villages to prepare for Sunday. The only people left with us were Peni, our builder, two local men and their families and a teenage boy named Meisi who had arrived one day on a small canoe and asked Peni if he could live with him.

As we settled into our own house we kept looking down towards the wharf

126

hoping that some of the village people might come to welcome us. We could not help contrasting with Saroa. No-one came.

On Sunday morning we decided to go to the nearest village, Karatiwo. Peni and Meisi, Bob and I squeezed into Meisi's canoe. It was very small and had no outrigger. I thought it would capsize with every movement. When we reached the village there was a great stretch of black, oozy mud between the river bank and the houses. We could see people sitting on a veranda looking at us.

I called out to them in Motu. 'My children, we are strangers here, will you help us?' Out they came, pulled the small canoe through the mud and up the bank. One man picked me up and carried me to the steps of the house. Up we climbed and others crowded into the house with us. We explained who we were and how we hoped to open up Veiru again, this time as a school for pastors.

When we asked if we could have a service with them they consented. Using Meisi's Kerewo (Aird Hill language) hymn book, we had a couple of hymns, then read a few Bible verses in Motu, told a Bible story and prayed. Then we talked some more, gave them some tobacco and said it was time to go. The men said, 'Not in that little canoe!' They got out one of their big canoes and Bob and I travelled home in style with six men to paddle. They came up to the house with us, talked some more and then went off. Now we had some friends.

That week the first four student families arrived on the boat with Pastor Bobby Peters and his wife and daughter. Soon we had our full complement of student families. Each house accommodated two families. Bob, Peni and the labourers worked hard to add shutters and doors, kitchens and pit toilets to each house.

Our first guest was Principal Raymond Perry who brought us greetings and gifts from Lawes' College. He brought not only money, but a beautiful Communion table cloth and the promise of a pastor to help, financed by the Suau District Church Council. What an encouragement!

I expect no college started with so little equipment — no building, no furniture and very little in the way of books or stationery. Our packing cases were turned into desks for the men. A friend from Camberwell, Melbourne, raised money which provided twenty metal-frame chairs, some blackboards, Bible maps and even sandfly nets for the student families. Our usual mosquito nets were no protection from the tiny sandflies.

Early in the year the Rankins' son, Bob, and his young wife Hilary, who had been married in Sydney, visited Bob's parents on their honeymoon. Bob worked for the Agriculture Department in Port Moresby.

By 29 March a classroom had been fashioned under the Rankins' house using woven sheets of sago midrib for the walls. The old school building had been refurbished and decorated with flowers ready for the opening ceremony. The building with its floor of mud, low walls of split nipa palm completed by a lattice of split pandanus, topped by a thatched roof, was a good lesson for the students in how to build an attractive building from local materials.

When John Cribb invited the Rankins to go with him to Goaribari Island at the mouth of the Kikori River, they had the opportunity to see a way of life which had changed little since Chalmers and Tomkins had been martyred in 1901. Sue tells the story:

There was a longhouse on the island about thirty metres in length. No women were allowed inside but things had changed, and I was allowed to go in and take a service. It was a strange feeling to be in this longhouse with the roof curved up at both ends. Down the centre was a long passage with cubicles opening onto both sides. Each cubicle belonged to a man and in it he kept all his hunting and dancing gear. At each end of the passage was a long table piled high with skulls. The old days were almost gone, but not quite.

By 1958 promiscuity and prostitution had taken toll of the Kerewo people through the introduction of venereal diseases. In his story *We Lived with Headhunters*, Ben Butcher describes the 'buguru' or marriage rites of the tribe which lasted three or four days and culminated in the bride being offered by her husband to every man in the dubu daimo, or longhouse, of his village. 'The next morning the two set off in their canoe for other villages where the same procedure was followed, and when at last they returned to their home, the girl would proudly display all she had won for herself and her man by her prostitution' (Hodder & Stoughton, London, 1963, p. 194).

These practices were the basis for the prostitution which was still rife in the 1960s. The men were taking their wives further and further afield, even to setting up a camp in Port Moresby.

In the 1920s Ben Butcher had tried to explain to the people what the results of their practices would be. Forty years later the Kerewo tribe had dropped from 10,000 to 2,000 people. Sue was very concerned for these women.

A short way downstream from Veiru was a trade store owned by John Senior, a very good friend of the Rankins'. When asked if the students could conduct a service each week for his workers, John offered the use of a dormitory which had just been completed.

When talking over their experiences on Sunday evening, the students who had visited Senior's store said they did not like preaching in the boy-house because in front of them was a table piled high with skulls. They asked if the skulls could be removed. Sue and Bob talked over asking John Senior to remove the skulls, and then decided that it was good for their students from other districts, where the old practices had died out, to see what the 'old days' were like. The skulls would remind them of what the Gospel could do to set people free. Within a short time the men told the missionaries that without a word being spoken, the skulls had been removed.

Pastor Bobby Peters and his wife started their second year at the college and a newly graduated couple from Lawes' College joined them, Pastor Sibona Mahuta and his wife Tau. Pastor Livingstone from Samoa came to help with the large building program and his wife Lili, a cousin of the Queen of Tonga, led the women, training them in sewing, handcraft, cooking and giving them Christian teaching.

A quote from Bob's 1959 report to P.D.C.: 'The arrival of Pastor Livingstone was a great blessing. For several weeks I was unable to do any outside work owing to illness. During this time Pastor Livingstone supervised the work (of building a lecture hall named the Oliver Tomkins Hall) in his own tireless way. His first big task with the help of Peni, the carpenter, and three labourers and with the students' help on non-school days, was to dismantle the old Technical shed, assemble the timbers, roofing iron and storey posts, in order, and then transfer them to a suitable spot on the narrow creek. Later we carried them to the site where the hall was to be erected. This was no small task for the posts were long and heavy. We had to call on extra help from the villages for the carrying up of the timbers. Once there the building was started'.

The hall was ready for opening by the Rev. Norman Cocks by the end of May. A food store, a storage shed near the wharf, and one of the new permanent houses for student families were completed that year. Livingstone's sense of humour helped when the work load was so heavy. He was a man of large proportions and his capacity for snoring was legendary throughout the campus.

Bob was very tired by the end of the year and he and Sue went on leave before the November P.D.C. meetings, so that they could be back in time to start the 1961 school year.

Chapter 17

Unexpected retirement?

Sue takes up the story:

After a couple of days in Sydney we went to Melbourne where Eve and Margaret were working. I was worried about Bob. He looked almost as grey as his suit, which had come out of mothballs for our leave.

During the first week a doctor visited us to give us a medical examination. He said Bob had angina of long standing and advised rest. How could I get Bob to rest? Two weeks later we took the morning service at Camberwell Church and in the evening went to Collins Street Independent Church in the City. Bob was anxious about being late and tried to hurry up the street at his normal pace. Some friends could see that he was not well and drove us home after the service.

On Monday Bob felt much better and we discussed offering to extend our period of service by two years. This would give five more years in which to see the college established. Tuesday Bob felt ill. The doctor came and prescribed some medicine and suggested Bob stay in bed for a while. He called in again early Wednesday morning.

We were expecting my sisters for afternoon tea but they were delayed, so I made tea and took a cup in to Bob who was in bed. We were sitting peacefully together when he gave a jerk and was gone. At that moment Eve and Margaret walked in. Should I have noticed something amiss? Should I have called the doctor? My sisters assured me that there was nothing I could have done.

Next morning the Nicholsons, my old friends from Kokebagu who now lived in Melbourne, came and took charge of many details. Eve was with me but Margaret, who was a private nurse, had gone back to her patient. Our son Bob flew down from Port Moresby.

In spite of my great grief and shock there was no release in tears. How could I find relief? Was I to be bereft of my husband and my life in Papua in one blow? The thought was unbearable.

The news of Bob Rankin's death reached Port Moresby just as the P.D.C. meetings were being completed. The missionaries met together and decided to ask Sue to return to Veiru with Sister 'Paul' Fairhall as her colleague till another appointment could be made. (Because of her deep aversion to her given name 'Constance', Sister Fairhall asked her colleagues to call her 'Paul'.) Sue was delighted to receive the invitation and also some letters from her students pleading with her to return and help them complete their course. Once again life was taking on some meaning. She would be able to continue the work that had meant so much to Bob and herself.

Since Paul Fairhall was not able to join Sue till April, Eve accompanied her to Veiru. John Cribb, who had been looking after the college, gave the two women a quiet welcome. To Sue the campus looked very beautiful. She was glad to be back with her beloved Papuan people.

John stayed on to help Sue. There were lots of jokes and laughs to help her along as she courageously struggled to get the lecture program going again for the students, who were so keen to complete their course. When Paul arrived in April the program of the college was able to go ahead. She took on all the medical work, the women's instruction and part of the men's lectures. There were so many children attending the primary school that the pastor and his wife and the teacher and his wife were all teaching. Sue supervised the store as well as doing most of the men's lectures.

At the end of the year Paul Fairhall returned to her work in Port Moresby. Because Ruatoka College was not yet completed, P.D.C. decided that Bob Beevers should conduct his teacher training course at Chalmers College for one year. Sue looked after her second-year students under the house and Bob used the Oliver Tomkins Hall.

Pastor Sibona and his wife stayed on and a teacher from Orokolo ran the school, which was used as a demonstration and practice school for the teacher trainees.

Margaret Beevers, a trained nurse, looked after the medical work and helped Sue with the housekeeping. Sue loved having their little children Christine and Andrew with her and helped Bob care for

131

them when Margaret went to Sydney for the birth of her third child, John.

In the four years since Sue and her husband had opened Chalmers College, the churches in the villages had been built up through the regular visits of the students. Forty-five people from the nearby villages had accepted Christ and joined the church. Forty-one were receiving instruction in the Seekers' Class. Thirty-five students and their wives had graduated from the college and their children had received primary education.

The women appreciated the training they had received. At an Easter service one woman said, 'It's not only our husbands who are called by God, we are called, too. Jesus needs us. When he was crucified where were the men? You know they all ran away but the women stayed. So we will stand and help our husbands to be strong and stand fast'.

The Rev. Laurie Gray visited the college in 1962. He had been chosen to succeed Sue as Principal. Sue knew that Laurie would continue to develop the vision she and Bob had had for the college and surrounding villages.

The Beevers and Sue spent Christmas at Veiru with three couples who had completed their pastor and teacher-training. They had stayed on to help Sue with the new student families who would arrive early in the new year. On Boxing Day Sue rose early. A dinghy was moving very swiftly downstream. It moved out of sight behind the river bank. Within a few minutes John Senior arrived at the door in great distress.

On Christmas afternoon he and his wife had gone to a plantation to visit, leaving the children in the care of their aunt. The children were playing hide-and-seek. They could not find two-year-old Robert. The parents came home to join the search. He was not found till next morning, wedged between the river bank and some boarding. His father had come to ask if the little one could be buried at Veiru.

There were some graves at Veiru, including that of Captain Andersen of the coastal vessel *The Papuan Chief*, but it had been decided that in future only people of the college family be buried there. What could Sue say to the parents in their grief? Of course she consented and poured out love and comfort on them. Bob Beevers and the students prepared for the burial beside the mission house. Sue led the service, full of grief herself for the bright little boy.

On the last day of January Sue farewelled the Beevers family and welcomed the Grays with their four small boys. For six weeks she worked with Laurie to start the students on their first year of study and then left to spend a fortnight with her son, Bob, his wife, Hilary, and their two children in Mount Hagen.

From mission to church

After thirty-eight years in Papua and now sixty-five years old, Sue felt that the time for her retirement was drawing near. She had been given two short assignments by P.D.C. First, to conduct an orientation course for five new missionaries, then to take part in a refresher course for six probationary pastors preparing for ordination.

Once again Sue found herself occupying the house on the Port Moresby mission station which had been her home for the first half of 1927. A great deal of thought had gone into the content of the orientation course. Sue had been asked to give the new recruits a good grounding in the Motu language. Then she planned to invite speakers who would give an overview of what was being done in Papua by various agencies. They heard representatives of various missions, Government departments, Guides, Scouts, YWCA and speakers on economic and social trends. It was an historical year, the first year of the new Papua Ekalesia. Missionaries were now the servants of the Papuan Church.

The aim of the London Missionary Society had always been to establish an indigenous church. At the end of World War II in 1949, a body of Papuan church leaders was formed to work alongside the missionaries' Papua District Committee in a consultative role. Each of the twelve districts was represented by one pastor and one deacon appointed for three years. The Papuan Church Assembly met annually.

Over the next ten years plans were discussed for the forming of an indigenous church. The suggested constitution written in 1959 provided for over three-quarters of the delegates to be nationals. The inauguration of the Papua Ekalesia took place on 21 November 1962, the anniversary of Lawes' landing in Port Moresby in 1874. The new church had the distinction of being the first major church to become independent in Papua New Guinea.

At the course there were stimulating discussions with the national pastors of the nearby villages and the new town of Koke. The first debate was on the place of the European minister in the new Papua Ekalesia. It was interesting that the pastors felt that the Europeans were needed in the church as district ministers. They also said that they would like some Europeans to volunteer for work as ministers of village congregations so that they could learn from the expatriates in this situation.

The new missionaries observed one of the Rev. Percy Chatterton's translation sessions when he was working on the Motu Old Testament. They visited the Christian Literature Crusade bookshop and attended some of the sessions of the Port Moresby District

Church Council. The course ended with a retreat conducted by Father Bryan of the Anglican Franciscan Order.

During the course, Sue took one week to attend the first women's conference of the Papua Ekalesia which was held at Hula. She had been invited to the conference as chaplain. How exciting to be part of a gathering of hundreds of women from all parts of Papua, meeting as Christians to encourage each other and learn together. The Gospel of Jesus Christ had brought many changes to the lives of women since Sue's first visit to Hula in 1926.

On her trip to Fife Bay at the beginning of August, Sue was accompanied by the Rev. Geoff and Mrs Shirley Ward, two of the new missionaries. The young pastors to be ordained had been Sue's students at Veiru. When someone teased Sue for being so short of stature, her ex-students sprang to her defence. It reminded Sue of a time at Saroa when the women were saying; 'Why aren't you tall like Sister Fairhall and Sister Phillips?' Sue apologised for her height and a widow threw her arms around her and exclaimed; 'We love you, even though you are only a threepenny bit!'

When Sue returned to Port Moresby after the refresher course, it seemed that her work in Papua had come to an end. She prepared to go to Melbourne with Bob and Hilary, who were going on leave.

That week in Port Moresby was a time of farewells for Gwen and Eric Ure, who were retiring to live in Brisbane. The Ures and the Rankins were 'neighbours' in adjoining districts for over thirty years, visiting each other, and acting as locum at leave times.

Sue says, 'As I stood on the wharf waving to Gwen I found my small grandson, at my side. "Your friend has gone, Nain," said he, taking my hand, "but you've got me, Nain." ("Nain" is Welsh for "Grandmother")'.

In 1964 Sue had one year's leave in Great Britain due to her. Her sister Margaret, who had moved to Melbourne years before, persuaded her to take it and the two sisters left by ship in May for Great Britain and returned early in January 1965. Sue, Eve and Margaret started looking for a house where they could settle together. A letter arrived from the secretary of the Papua Ekalesia asking Sue to go to Moru while the Rev. Bert Brown was on leave. Her sisters laughed at Sue's excitement. It was plain to see that her heart was in Papua. They agreed that she must go. She insisted on staying to complete the house-hunting and buying of furniture, but a week after her sisters had moved into the house, Sue left for Sydney and Port Moresby.

The days when the only transport to Gabagaba and Rigo was a weekly coastal boat or a canoe had passed since Sue left Saroa in 1956. She could never bear to return to visit her beloved people and district but, after her arrival in Port Moresby, Bob Beevers arrived by truck and persuaded Sue to visit the Ruatoka Teachers' College which had been built at Kwikila. Bob drove along the coastal road to Gabagaba and then inland through Rigo, the old government station, past Gomore, Kwalimurubu, Saroa and Gidobada to the new Government station at Kwikila and the college. It was a beautiful campus and Sue was very impressed with the progress made in her old district. Her vision of having a centre nearer to the inland population centres had been brought into being by the government and, in the form of a teachers' college, by the church.

On her return trip Sue still felt that she could not bear to stop and greet her old friends at Saroa but Bob prevailed on her to stop at the new government school, Dauma Gini, which had been built on a hillside south of the village, the traditional site of the legend of the giant and the twin boys. The headmaster escorted Sue to each classroom and had her say a few words to each class. She found that her Sinaugoro primer was still in use and that she was remembered as the 'mother of all the Sinaugoro people'.

At Moru Sue was welcomed in the service on Sunday morning with, 'Last time you came here you took our missionary away'. Sue replied with due humility that she was sorry but had come to help them now if they would allow her. The people laughed and forgave her and Sue took up the threads of a district missionary's responsibility once again.

Sue had just started work at Moru when news arrived of her sister Margaret's death. She had been crossing the street on her way to church with Eve when she was struck by a car, and did not recover. It was impossible for Sue to reach Melbourne in time for the funeral. After the sad telegram Sue received several very happy letters from Margaret written during her last weeks.

When Bert Brown returned at the end of the year, Sue went to P.D.C. again expecting to be retired. She found that the Grays had left Veiru because of Mrs Gray's ill health. Again Sue was invited to return to Chalmers College.

'Lord, we need someone to teach us about you, will you please send Sinabada Rankin back to us,' prayed the chief of Babaguina village, downstream from Veiru. Later one of his people said, 'God has answered your prayer. Did you know that Mrs Rankin came back this afternoon?'

It has been said of the delta people that the mud had seeped into their very souls. It is an area of endemic malaria and many other parasites that cause chronic anaemia. The people lacked vitality and initiative. Since Chalmers College had opened in 1956, the regular Sunday visits, access to medical care and school for their children, and the love and release from fear that the Gospel brings had changed the attitude of the people. They responded to the love

135

of Christ in Sue, knowing that she respected them, and they could trust her. She was so happy to be back, not only at the helm of the college, but planning new ways to show the Love of Christ to the people of the villages and Government station.

Her first need was for a load of firewood. She sent a message to Tipeiewo village. Her colleagues were amazed that within a short time a canoe load of cut logs was waiting at the wharf. 'How do you do it?' they asked. From the days of building the house at Saroa, Sue had the ability to sit patiently and talk to the people, understand how they were thinking, and convince them of her love and concern for them. They responded by caring for her as their mother. She arranged for the people to supply timber for the building and maintenance program of the college, always paying fairly and promptly.

The work of the college was again divided up amongst the staff provided: a deaconess, a builder and his teacher-wife, and Peni and Waime. Pastor Sibona Mahuta was Sue's assistant-principal.

Throughout the delta the search for oil and natural gas was continuing. Millions of dollars worth of equipment was brought in and accommodation built for the workers. When the search in each area was complete, the camp was abandoned. It was possible to get permission from the oil companies to remove building materials or useful fittings and machinery. During their Christmas break Sue sent students who had completed first year to a nearby camp to salvage timber and roofing iron.

They took tools, plenty of rations and tobacco, and shotgun and cartridges and led by Peni and Waime, went off by canoe up the Kikori River. It was eerie to walk through the deserted camp with its almost-new buildings taken over by the jungle. Hibiscus had pushed up through the concrete floors and were already two metres high. The camp had the feeling of being peopled by the ghosts of the geologists and engineers and others who had staffed it so recently. The team worked hard and, when the *Tamate* arrived, were able to load many sheets of iron and pieces of hardwood timber which would make for much more permanent buildings at Veiru.

The 1967 school year started with twenty-seven student families, but Sue found that attitudes were very different. She was faced with her first student strike! Sue handled it well, calmly but firmly. The college community was soon working well together again.

But there had been a coastal steamer at the wharf in Veiru at the time of the strike, and the story had travelled to Port Moresby. Just when Sue had felt the whole episode was over, she received worried letters from some of her colleagues, fearing that there had been violence! Sue was able to reassure them that all was well.

At the P.D.C. meeting in November 1967 Sue asked that a new principal be appointed to Chalmers College. She had been in Papua forty-one years and felt once again that she should hand over her position to a man. The Rev. Geoff Ward and his wife Shirley were appointed to the college.

When Shirley and Geoff arrived in January, Sue stayed on to hand over, moving in to share Rhoda Vicker's house for the remainder of her time at the college. She says, 'I have often regretted the fact that after a couple of years Chalmers College was closed and taken to Lawes' College. That in turn was shortly closed, and all training transferred to Rabaul. Ruatoka College was closed and combined with Gaulim Teachers' College in Rabaul. Soon there were no colleges in Papua at all'. The mission still conducted a primary school at Veiru and a boys vocational school which taught boys after grade six skills that would be useful in the village or in small businesses. However, the fruit of the work of Chalmers College is still going on in the work of the pastors who were trained to work in difficult conditions among disadvantaged people.

When Sue left Veiru for the last time, the Aird Hills mission station had been moved to Kapuna, adjacent to the mission hospital on the banks of the Pia River. John Cribb and Dr Peter Calvert could see that Sue did not wish to leave Papua. The needs of their district were very great and they felt that her experience and wisdom should not be wasted. They asked Sue to join them.

Chapter 18

A new ministry

Peter and John had recently visited a group of villages many kilometres up the Purari River, just below the Hatha Gorge. Peter visited Lake Tebera, where the houses nestled among the reeds of the lake. These people were reputed to be cannibals and headhunters, and had threatened to kill the next patrol officer who came along. John went to some villages further downstream, arranging for Peter to pick him up in the launch on a certain day. At each village the men passed through, the people received them hospitably and appeared amazed that they had not been killed and eaten at the previous village!

It was a beautiful part of the country, with a very swift-flowing river and a rainfall of 12,500 millimetres (500 inches) a year. The people were short, stocky, dark highlanders. The people of the villages pleaded with the two missionaries to send them someone who would tell them the Good News.

Meanwhile, a rumour had reached Kapuna, and the anxiously waiting wives, that Peter and John had been killed. Two days later the men arrived home to a very warm welcome from Lin Calvert and Hazel Cribb! Sue, on hearing of the needs of the people, was very eager to go and live with them. She said, 'If I die there, I die. What does it matter where I die?'

The offer was discussed with some men from Uraru and Lake Tebera, who were visiting Kapuna hospital. They were very enthusiastic and went home to build a house for Sue and level the ground for an airstrip near the village.

Sue arrived from Veiru in John Senior's dinghy, prepared to go to the upper Purari. A Missionary Aviation Fellowship cessna was to take Sue to see the place and meet the people, and then on to Mount Hagen to spend a short holiday with Bob and Hilary and her grandchildren. Peter and John met her at Baimuru looking very glum. A letter had arrived from the Rev. Bill Bache, secretary of the Papua Ekalesia, refusing permission for Sue to live in such an isolated spot. The plane was waiting. As she climbed aboard John and Peter said, 'Don't worry, leave it to us'.

When the plane landed at Uraru, the people of the village were eagerly waiting to meet Sue. They showed her the house they had built for her and introduced her to the two little boys who were to help her in the house. The villagers were very proud of their airstrip and asked when she would return to live with them. It was very, very hard for Sue to say, 'I don't know when I will be back,' and board the plane for the flight to Mount Hagen.

After visiting her family, Sue went on to Port Moresby to plead with the mission leaders to be allowed to settle in that village. 'I am retired, it doesn't matter where I live. I could do so much for those people; they are expecting me'. But it was no use.

John Cribb says, 'I still wonder what might have happened if Sue had gone there. It could have been a disaster; it could have been the making of the place. Later Missionary Aviation Fellowship float planes were used so the airstrip wasn't really necessary. The planes could tie up in a little cove out of the mainstream of the river. Later a Samoan pastor was appointed to the area'.

Meanwhile John and Peter had been adjusting their plans for Sue. If she could not go to the upper Purari they would build a house for her at Baimuru, the government station on the banks of the Purari River. As well as the government office and airstrip, there was a small hospital manned by medical orderlies, a boarding school of about 200 boys and a few girls, a saw mill and a gaol. Sue would be the chaplain for the school and pastor to the people of Baimuru, people from many parts of Papua and New Guinea. Some were Christians who needed encouragement and teaching.

Some of the school staff and their wives were Christians and soon Sue had a church service going each Sunday in one of the school classrooms. Before the church service, one of the teachers, who was a Lutheran, and his wife helped Sue with Sunday school. During the afternoon Sue held a boys' Bible class, and later in the day went to the gaol to visit the prisoners, have a short service with them, and give them some of her scones.

Sue felt that some of the people from the sawmill were not very happy about having a missionary in Baimuru. There were some heavy drinkers among the population and an application for a tavern had been made. Sue and Peter appealed to the liquor licensing tribunal without success. Peter could foresee trouble for the little settlement of Baimuru.

She was concerned about the women who lived at the sawmill. Taken out of their village, where they worked hard in the garden or making sago, to a place where their husbands worked for cash, they had very little to do. Most of them had not had much opportunity to go to school or learn how to care for their children and homes. With the help of her companion Kamaro and some of the teachers' wives, Sue started a women's club.

Most afternoons Sue and her helpers would go up to the playing field near the sawmill and play the same games she had used in her efforts to get to know the women of the mountains in the Saroa district. Gradually the wives of the sawmill workers joined in. In spite of the great pain of rheumatism in her feet, Sue led them enthusiastically in the games. When the sawmill workers' wives became used to the energetic missionary and her helpers, the teachers' wives suggested that they meet near Sue's house so that she would not have the long walk to the sawmill.

Each gathering started with devotions and then went on to sewing and other activities. The sawmill manager's daughter came to help Sue, teaching the women to sew garments on their own hand-sewing machines. Little tables for the machines were made from cases retrieved from the oil search camps. Friends in Australia sent wool and cloth.

Among the women who came to the club were a few who were rather dirty and unkempt. They would come for a few weeks and then disappear. Sue was curious. She asked the others whether the husbands had stopped working at the sawmill. The women replied that those husbands did not work at the sawmill. They brought their wives to Baimuru to work as prostitutes, and after a few weeks, took them home again. Sue was surprised that the Baimuru women did not resent them. They said, 'It's nothing to do with the women. It's their husbands' business. They have no choice'. The women were accepted into the club and shown friendship while they were there.

At that time in Papua there was a lot of talk about keeping the old customs and remembering the old culture. Sue spent many hours discussing with the church members which customs were good and should be observed. The women's club had outgrown Sue's cottage and she suggested to the church members that they build a shed that could be used for the many activities she was planning for the community.

As soon as the shed was completed the men started to use it on Friday nights for games: pingpong, darts, memory, Monopoly. The teachers were glad of a place where they could have some recreation. The women used it for their club activities. Some of the school girls joined in and after handcraft, helped Kamaro make a cup of tea for the women. Rather than take the food offered and go home, Sue taught the women to sit and eat a piece of cake and drink a cup of tea. They then went outside and played games.

The leaders of the women's club decided to have a competition to see who kept the cleanest and most attractive house. The women took great pleasure in having a cloth on a small table and a jar made into a vase holding flowers on it. Each Saturday the women divided up into two teams. The teachers' wives went in one direction to inspect the houses, and the sawmill workers' wives went in the other direction.

The pupils were not permitted to take the books from the very small school library to the dormitories so Sue, wanting to encourage them to read, set up a lending library in her house. With the help of the Red Cross, Mount Gravatt Congregational Church in Brisbane and her own family she soon had a good selection. There was a constant stream of boys and girls exchanging their library books. When the teachers wanted to purchase school textbooks Sue ordered them from Port Moresby.

In spite of the appeal a tavern and hotel opened in Baimuru. The men gravitated to the pub because there was nothing to do at weekends. So Sue started a soccer competition among the teachers, sawmill workers and older school boys. When she could not get anyone to organise the games she did it herself, teaching the men the rules. Before long she had them calling in at her cottage for a chat, asking her advice about many things.

The night of the official opening of the hotel, Sue's friends from the sawmill invited her to go with them to the opening and dinner. The bar had been open all day and some of the men were drunk. One man walked past with a glass in his hand and bumped into Sue. Someone shouted, 'You look where you go. You no bump mother belong all of us!' After dinner Sue excused herself. She walked home with her heart aching to see the people she loved so much the worse for drink.

The congregation grew till all the school teachers and their wives and children were attending services. Some of the sawmill workers also started to come. There were people who were church members in their home villages but had lost interest since coming to Baimuru. They had come back and some new people came as well. A cup of tea in Sue's house after church helped her to get to know the newcomers.

Sue's time at Baimuru came to an end when she received an urgent radio message; 'Your son has had a serious heart attack. He is going to Sydney for by-pass surgery'. Sue hastily packed and joined her family in Port Moresby, saying very brief farewells to all her friends in Baimuru. She says;

I hadn't done much there at all. I had no special job but had been happy to point to the Lord, who is always near to help and save. Years later I received a letter from one of the schoolboys thanking me for 'the good food you gave us, teaching us about God our Father, Jesus our Saviour, and the Holy Spirit'.

Chapter 19

Farewell

The year 1972 saw the celebration of the centenary of the arrival of the first L.M.S. missionaries in Papua New Guinea. Sue was awarded an M.B.E., and Percy Chatterton an O.B.E. (He was to be knighted in 1981). Sue's investiture at Government House, Port Moresby, was delayed because she was in Sydney with Bob at the time. When he had recovered from his surgery, she returned with Bob and Hilary to Papua New Guinea, this time to settle with them in Port Moresby.

With Bob working at the Agriculture Department and Hilary at the Health Department, Sue kept house for them. But characteristically, Sue soon found more work to do. The Rankins' house was within walking distance of a hospital where Sue spent many hours visiting the patients.

She often recognised people from the places where she had worked. At that time Chrissie Chatterton — Percy's wife — was there, helpless after a stroke. She had spent many years serving the people of Papua New Guinea. She had asked to be buried at Delena, where she had been very happy. Sue, Bob and Hilary accompanied Percy to her funeral.

While visiting the hospital one day Sue heard a conversation from the other side of the ward. An old man was saying, 'That's Miselesi (Miss Ellis)'. A younger man was contradicting him. Sue walked across the ward. 'Yes, I'm Miss Elesi'. The younger man said, 'No you're not, you're Mrs Rankin'. Sue replied, 'Yes, but when I was young I was Miss Elesi'.

The young man exclaimed, 'The same person! The old people talk about Miss Elesi, we talk about Mrs Rankin. I didn't know it was the same person!' Sue discovered that they came from Gamoga, the village of the episode about 'piribou' or pants. They told her that the church in Gamoga was thriving.

An annual festival was started in Port Moresby to commemorate those great trading voyages undertaken by the Motu men to the Gulf in the days of the sailing canoe. Many schools took part in the celebrations. As Sue watched the dancing, a teacher spoke to her. His father had been one of the Ikeaga boys who had accompanied Sue on her first patrols. He said, 'A white woman came to me. She was very angry. She said, "Why did those missionaries put a stop to this dancing?" ' Sue asked, 'What did you say?' He answered; 'I said, "I'm sorry madam, but you are labouring under a misapprehension. It was not the missionaries who stopped this dancing but our fathers. They did it because it always caused trouble in our villages".'

Ron Lean had for many years befriended the Saroa men who went to Port Moresby to work. He led a Motu service at Boroko United Church and a Bible study for the Saroa district men in his home. When Sue became a resident of Port Moresby, he invited her to take the service and lead the Bible study. Again Sue was doing what she loved most, teaching from the Bible.

Percy Chatterton (and his translation team) had completed his revision of the New Testament and translation of the Old Testament into Motu. At last Sue could give a Bible study on the Prophets. The language used in the translation was the more stable 'classical Motu' of the old days and of the Saroa district. The Motu of the Port Moresby district varied from village to village and was constantly changing because of the cosmopolitan nature of the town.

Unfortunately, many of the younger Motuans found the 'pure' Motu of the new translation very difficult whereas Sue was interested to find that the Saroa men in the class knew the more difficult Motu words, and could give her the equivalent in Sinaugoro. Sue was reminded of the Rev. R. L. Turner's advice to her when she first started learning Motu, that the Sinaugoro people, who used it as a second language, spoke purer Motu based on the language of the New Testament.

In 1976 Bob and Hilary decided to move to Brisbane. The veteran missionary had one more small task to complete before she joined them. She had been asked to write a booklet in Motu, an introduction to the books of the Bible. Sue stayed on with Margaret Peterson who was working as Education Secretary for the United

Church and Nita Tobin, who was the business manager of the United Church. Margaret assisted Sue by typing the book ready for publication.

Before Hilary left for Australia she drove Sue to Kwalimurubu to take a Communion service in the church she had opened two years previously. A very beautiful garden had been planted round the church. It was tended by the families of the church for a month in turn. At the end of the main service, before Communion, the people performed a ceremony for Sue. The senior deacon came forward and presented her with a drum. 'Dr Lawes came to visit us often, but we did not listen, Mr Turner came but we still did not listen, but then you came, you were only a girl, but you broke our drum'. The big dance and feast for which the people used to prepare for months was called the Gaba or drum feast. It was the symbol of the old way which they now called the Way of Darkness whereas the Christian way is the Way of Light. Then a younger deacon came forward and presented Sue with a Bible, saying that it was with the Bible that she had broken their drum.

At that time the old deacon, Vere, was still alive. He reminded Sue that when he married the daughter of the first deacon, Guguna Kevau, he had not been interested in becoming a Christian. He said, 'When my son, Guguna Vere, was born you and Taubada Rankin came to baptise him. I did not bother to come back from the garden. You gave my wife a message for me. You said, "Tell Vere if he loves his baby son, he will walk before him in the Way of Light". I listened to that word and decided to follow Jesus'.

Soon after the visit to Kwalimurubu the people of the Saroa District invited Sue to the Synod meeting which was being held at Saroa. In Sue's words:

What a lovely ending it was! First of all the Headmaster and staff of the Administration school brought all the older classes to see me and sing for me. They also brought me a present. Then I spoke at the opening service of the Synod and Communion. My voice is not strong these days but I did my best. Then we had a meal together and speeches and gifts from each part of the district. Papuan people are always generous and they gave me over 200 dollars as well as traditional gifts of bags and lime gourds.

Pastor Raka Daba, healed of cancer, who had been one of my first schoolboys at Kalaigoro, walked with me to the end of the village. He said, 'Our mother, go in peace, don't worry, the work has been well established'. He kissed me and I left.

Sue left Papua in 1976, a few months after Bob and Hilary. She settled in Mount Gravatt, Brisbane, with her sister Eve, where she still lives.

Postscript

by Sue Rankin

When we desired to bring people to new life in Christ, I think in some ways we were wrong in stressing sin. Because Christ came to bring something far more than freedom from sin. People who are not Christians don't have a sense of sin, so there is no real point of contact there. In Papua, it was no use talking about sin at first because the people did not know anything about sin. When they came into the church they started to grasp the ideas of justification and peace and grace. We missionaries talked to the people most about fear, about bad spirits and the Good Spirit.

Nowadays I think we should stress the kind of living that Christ brings. He came to give us Life, more abundant Life, Life in all its fulness. Freedom from sin is part of this, but we are not conscious of it till we become Christians. We need to talk about the fulness of life that Christ gives, and that's what we did in Papua. If you come to listen to this Good News, it brings you a new kind of life. That's what the people believed. They said they had been living in the dark and the Gospel came and gave them Light.

Christ brought them freedom from fear; fear of sorcery, fear of spirits. Every rock had its spirit, every tree, every creek, every river had a kind of spirit. Remember the story of old Nou Airi when he had thrashed his wife and thought he had killed her? He was out in the bush that night, hiding, full of remorse and full of fear because he said there was nobody there, no-one to help him. The spirits were all around him in the bush. Then he remembered in his despair, as the mosquitoes and other insects made his life miserable, that his pastor had said, 'God listens to prayer and answers it'.

146

Nou Airi said there was no-one to help him, so he prayed to God. The people were not conscious of sin, only sorry when they were found out, like Nou Airi on this occasion, full of remorse. He hadn't meant to hurt his wife.

The penny doesn't drop when we talk to people outside the church about sin. They don't think of the things they are doing as sin. When we become Christians we realise that the things we are doing are against God's will. Unless we know God how can we talk about sin? When the Papuan people talk about repenting, they talk about 'helalo kerehai' or right about face, turning away from sin to turn towards God. That's when they understand righteousness and grace and peace and hope.

God is so full of generosity and love, he wants to give everyone, no matter how bad, abundant Life. In Wales we say that God gives with his left hand, he gives to everybody, health, this lovely world. But there are gifts God reserves for those who seek him. The gifts that we ask him for are the gifts of God's right hand. With his left hand he is always giving, but there are some things he keeps for those who seek.

In Welsh we have an ordinary word for peace meaning peacefulness, absence of war, 'heddwch'. But the one the angels sang about, peace on earth, is 'tangnefedd', the word Jesus used when he said, 'My peace I give you'. When we talk about the gospel of peace we say 'efengyl tangnefedd' (evangel of peace). The first peace is between people and nations but 'tangnefedd' you can't have without God. It comes from God and can overflow us, like shalom.

The most important thing I would like to say is that the only thing in the whole world that can change people and really make them whole and vital is the story of our Lord with the ever-present helping power of the Holy Spirit. My favourite text is 2 Corinthians 5:17 (NEB): 'When anyone is united to Christ, there is a new world; the old order has gone, and a new order has already begun'. That is true. I've seen it happen time after time.